VERONIKA LINDBERG

Effortless Patterns
by Kutova Kika

KNITS TO WEAR

Hardie Grant
BOOKS

Veronika Lindberg, also known as Kutova Kika, is an internationally acclaimed knitwear designer. She is known for her modern, Scandinavian-inspired designs that combine comfort and contemporary elegance. With more than 500,000 active followers on her social media channels and many appearances in major international media outlets, including *The New York Times*, her work inspires knitters around the world to create effortlessly stylish knits.

CONTENTS

PREFACE

When designing the knits for this book, I had two guiding questions in mind: 'Which of my hand-knitted items do I wear most often?' and 'What do I find most enjoyable to knit?'

These questions have prompted me to take an honest look at what I actually wear in my everyday life: Which knits do I wear on repeat and what do I feel most comfortable in? As we all know, when you feel good in your clothes, you radiate confidence.

I've always loved putting together different outfits and expressing myself through the clothes I wear and make. Over the years, my style has evolved a lot – from idolising Audrey Hepburn's clean and ultra-elegant style to my boho hippie-chic days as an art student (which, to be honest, often weren't that chic).

Two things have always been close companions in my style journey: colours and textures. I love playing with unexpected combinations when putting together outfits, willing to take a bit of a risk in the face of the fear of standing out from the crowd or someone not 'getting it'. Of course, this approach has led to a whole bunch of clown-like costumes, too – I've not always totally nailed 'unconventional-but-in-a-cool-and-fashion-trailblazing-way'.

Looking effortlessly chic can take a surprising amount of effort, after all.

In recent years, two new aspects have become part of my style journey: materials and details. Or you could say I've become a lot more picky. Gone are the days of buying cheap acrylic knits from fast-fashion brands to get that rush of dopamine that a new piece of clothing can provide. Ah, all the promises that fresh and brilliant outfits seem to hold – a whole new persona with an exciting new life! Today, I'm wiser and I spend all my money in yarn shops buying expensive yarn instead ... well, I'm not sure I've become that much wiser, come to think of it, but at least it's a lot more sustainable and yarn doesn't go out of style as quickly.

So, I've tried to shift my focus to being more intentional with my style choices, which has led me to focus on value, but what does that even mean?

Well, I think one way to measure the value of a piece of clothing is in how much it gets worn. My best pieces of clothing are the ones I reach for the most: you don't get much value out of something that never gets worn, right?

In my lifetime, I've probably knitted more than a hundred sweaters and cardigans, but that doesn't mean that I've loved or worn them equally. To be honest, some of them I've only worn a few times!

Now, you might think 'what a waste after spending all of that time and effort!' and at some point, I might have felt the same way. But now, I think it's all just part of the process of finding your style, what you like to wear and what feels most like you.

This book is called *Knits to Wear* because that's what I hope they will be: knits that you'll want to wear again and again, for many years to come.

In this book, you'll find patterns ranging from simple and timeless basic knits (e.g., the *Simple Things* and *Coffee Run* sweaters) to modern pieces with romantic twists (e.g., the *Take Me Out* and *Urban Romance* sweaters) to projects with decorative structures (e.g., the *My Favourite Story* and *Sweetheart* sweaters) to more traditional colourwork knits (e.g., the *Playful Palette* sweater and *Daily Stripes* cardigan).

I've designed these knits with both the journey and the end goal in mind: projects that are enjoyable to knit and will feel good to wear.

While making this book, I also became a mother, which means that a sense of no-fuss, casual elegance has become a huge value in my work as a knit designer. I want my style to feel put together and as though I made an effort, without actually having to make that much of an effort.

I've included styling tips and ideas to inspire you to create knits that reflect your personal style and bring you joy when you wear them. Whether you are a beginner or an experienced knitter, there is something for everyone in these pages. I believe that the process of creating with your own hands is not just what you produce but about the journey of making something with love and care.

So, grab your needles, pick out some beautiful yarn, and let's embark on this knitting journey together. May these knits become cherished pieces that you reach for time and time again, bringing you comfort, confidence, and a sense of style that is uniquely you.

– *Kika*

One thing's for sure when it comes to knitting: there isn't one right way to do things, there are a whole lot of different ways. The internet is full of advice (I've got a YouTube channel with lots of tips and tutorials), and as a general rule I'd say: do what works for you. That being said, for this book I wanted to share a few tips that I've discovered and incorporated into my own knitting over the years.

10 TIPS TO KNIT LIKE A PRO

1. TRY IT ON AS YOU GO

Want to make sure your knit project fits just right? Try it on while it's still on your needles! As most of the patterns in this book are top-down, it's super easy to check the fit as you go. Just slide your stitches onto a stitch holder or some scrap yarn, and slip on your work-in-progress to assess it. This way, you can tweak the body and sleeve lengths to match your style perfectly. While each pattern provides suggested lengths, don't hesitate to adjust these to your liking – you might prefer sleeves that extend slightly over your wrists or something shorter. The beauty of making your own clothes is that you can tailor them to suit your body and style perfectly.

2. GIVE YOUR KNITS A DAY AT THE SPA

Sure, knitting the piece is a big deal, but the magic really happens in the finishing touches. Enter: blocking.

I've not included separate blocking instructions for each of the patterns in this book, but I highly recommend that you take the time to give your knit a spa day at the end of the process. You're going to wet or steam it, shape it to perfection, and let it dry. Think of it as a way to iron out those little glitches and give your project that polished, 'I totally know what I'm doing' look.

Blocking is especially crucial for showing off lace patterns, cables and colourwork. It helps open up the stitches and reveals all those intricate details that were hiding in the shadows, like a surprise twist in your favourite show.

Now, let's talk tools – you don't need to go full-on MacGyver, but you might want to invest in a few essentials to make the job easier. Consider getting some designated blocking mats, rust-proof pins and either a spray bottle or a steam iron. If you're working with delicate fabrics, blocking wires are your new best friend as they'll give you perfectly straight edges.

Here's how it's done: Give your knit a gentle soak in cold or lukewarm water, with an optional splash of wool wash. Make sure the entire garment is fully soaked and let it sit for 10–15 minutes. Squeeze out the excess water (gently, no wringing – your knit isn't a dish towel!). Then, lay it out flat to dry and shape it to match your pattern's measurements.

Or, you can try steam-blocking. If you don't own a steamer you can use an iron instead: soak a kitchen towel, place it over your knit and gently press with the iron to allow steam to open up and smooth out the fabric.

Putting in the time to finish your knits properly means they'll look polished and professional, so go on, give your knits the love they deserve!

3. JOIN NEW YARN MORE SMOOTHLY

So, you're happily knitting along, and suddenly, bam! You're out of yarn. No need to panic —there are a few ways to join that new skein and keep the knitting train rolling.

First up, the classic 'leave a tail' method. This is where you leave a few inches of both the old and new yarn, then weave those ends in when you're all done. It's like leaving a secret trail of breadcrumbs that you'll tidy up later. Sure, it works, but let's be honest – it's a bit of a procrastinator's move.

Then there's the 'spit splice' technique, which is as delightful (or icky) as it sounds.

This one's for the animal fibre lovers. You literally spit (or if you're more civilised, use water) on the ends of the yarns, rub them together like you're trying to start a fire, and boom – they magically fuse! It's like a yarn wizard's spell, but with a bit of spit. This technique is strong, seamless, and a bit of a party trick to impress your knitting buddies.

But let's get real – the quickest and easiest way (which I use all the time) is to just tie a knot. Yup, nothing fancy, just a good ol' double knot. Tie it tight, make sure it's secure, and keep knitting like nothing happened. Just be sure to work the knot so that it stays on the wrong side of the fabric, out of sight. It's fast, it's easy, and it gets the job done – kind of like the fast food of yarn joining. Sure, the purists might gasp, but hey, if it works, it works!

In the end, whether you're a weaver, a splicer, or a knot-tier, the best technique is the one that keeps you happily knitting along without missing a stitch.

4. WEAVE IN THE ENDS AS YOU GO

If you struggle to find the motivation to weave in all those pesky ends when you're finished with a project, I totally get it – finishing a project can sometimes feel like trying to muster up the energy to do laundry after a holiday. That's why I recommend weaving them in as you go. Not only does this keep your project looking tidy (perfect for those Instagram-worthy work-in-progress shots), but it also means you're not left with a mountain of ends to deal with when you could be done. Plus, it helps me avoid the dreaded 'I'll finish it later' pile that we all know never sees the light of day again!

5. REMEMBER THE MAGIC OF THE FINISHING TOUCHES!

I've learned that those finishing touches – evenly bound-off edges, a crisp button band, or a perfectly neat collar—are what truly elevate a hand-knitted piece from homemade to a handmade masterpiece. In fact, I have a few knits tucked away in my wardrobe that I don't wear as much as I'd like, all because I skipped some key finishing steps and didn't go back to fix them.

Putting in the effort to nail those final details is absolutely worth it. Not only does this give your project a polished, professional look, but it's also incredibly rewarding to see your hard work come together in such a complete way. I once re-knit a collar four or five times just to get the stitch count and fit exactly right, and let me tell you, that persistence paid off. The difference between 'good enough' and 'just right' can turn a piece you like into a piece you love – and one you'll actually want to wear. So, embrace the finishing process as part of the journey, not just the end, and your knits will shine for it.

6. FIX A SLOPPY COLLAR

If the collar on your sweater is too loose and flares out, there's an easy fix. Sew a clear elastic thread into the collar and gently tighten it. This invisible thread, commonly used in jewellery-making, blends seamlessly with the knitted fabric, giving your collar a snug fit without altering the look of your garment.

7. SOFTEN ITCHY KNITS

If you find your yarn is a bit too scratchy, give it a soak in a bath with a small amount of hair conditioner. This helps soften the fibres, making the garment more comfortable to wear. Here's how to do it: Fill a basin with lukewarm water and add a small amount of hair conditioner or a dedicated wool wash designed to soften fibres. Submerge the knit in the mixture and let it soak for about 15–30 minutes. After soaking, gently squeeze out the water (do not wring) and rinse the knit in clean water. Lay it flat to dry, reshaping as needed.

8. STORE YOUR KNITS SMARTER

To keep your knits looking their best, it's a good idea to store them folded rather than hanging. Handmade knits can be heavy, so if you leave them hanging, they might stretch out and lose their shape over time. But if you love the way knits look on hangers, there's a hack for that! Just fold them in half vertically and hang them from the armpit area. This way, they stay in shape, and you still get to enjoy seeing them in your closet. It's a win-win for your wardrobe and your knitting efforts!

9. A QUICK GUIDE TO MASTER YARN WEIGHTS

When you're diving into the world of knitting, understanding yarn weights is like learning the language of knitters – essential and surprisingly fun! Yarn weight refers to the thickness of the yarn and helps determine the size and drape of your finished piece.

Each pattern in this book states the specific yarn weight needed for it and also which yarns the samples were knitted with. You can always substitute the yarns mentioned in the pattern, but you'll need to choose a yarn with a similar weight.

Use this handy little guide when choosing the yarn for your project:

Lace (600–800 m / 660–880 yds per 100 g): These are your delicate, dainty yarns – think of them as the ballerinas of the knitting world. Perfect for airy and light-as-a-feather knits. In this book you'll often find that a strand of lace weight yarn, specifically silk mohair, is combined with other fibres to add a subtle sheen and fuzziness to the fabric.

Fingering (400–500 m / 440–550 yds per 100 g): Fingering is thinner than a sport weight yarn but thicker than lace, making it ideal for lightweight garments. Think of it as the yarn that gives you that perfect touch of warmth without the bulk, and it's great for showing off detailed stitchwork.

Sport & DK (200–300 m / 220–330 yds per 100 g): DK weight yarn can feel to a knitter like the perfect bed in the Goldilocks tale – not too thick, not too thin, but just right, making it suitable for a wide range of projects. Sport weight is a touch lighter, great for garments that aren't too bulky.

Worsted & Aran (100 m / 110 yds per 100 g): These yarns are the reliable work-horses of the knitting world. Worsted and aran weight yarns are the sweet spot for beginners – they are easy to work with and give satisfying, quick results.

Bulky (50 m / 55 yds per 100 g): Bulky or chunky yarn often knits up very fast. It's perfect when you want to make cosy pieces or to create a dense fabric for added structure.

Remember, the weight of your yarn affects the size of your project, so match it with the pattern's recommendations or adjust your needles to get the right fit. And don't be afraid to experiment and combine different weights and fibres – half the fun of knitting is in the exploration!

10. USE STICKY NOTES AND WASHI TAPE

Washi tape and sticky notes can be your best buddies when it comes to following a pattern (I have an entire drawer dedicated to cute washi tapes). Use washi tape to mark your current row or section – it's repositionable, so you can move it as you go, keeping your place without leaving permanent marks. Sticky notes are great for jotting down reminders or making notes on adjustments, and you can put them directly onto your pattern. By combining these tools, you'll stay organised, reduce mistakes, and add a bit of fun to your knitting process.

Give my tips a try and see the difference they make!

ABBREVIATIONS

BOR beginning of round

CC contrasting colour

Dec decrease

DPN double pointed needle

DS double stitch (used when working German Short Rows, see special techniques)

est established

Inc increase

GSR German Short Rows

K knit

K2tog Knit 2 stitches together through the front loops. 1 stitch decreased.

K3tog Knit 3 stitches together through the front loops. 2 stitches decreased.

Kfb Knit the stitch through the front and back. First insert the right needle in the stitch on the left needle and knit as you would normally but don't drop the stitch from your left needle. Next bring your right needle to the back of the left needle and knit into the same stitch through the back. Slip the stitch from the left needle to the right. 1 stitch increased.

LC left cross cable

m marker

MC main colour

M1L Make 1 left (left-leaning increase), knit] the strand between 2 sts by inserting the left needle from front to back and knit the stitch twisted (through the back loop). 1 stitch increased.

M1Lp Make 1 left purl (left-leaning increase), purl the strand between 2 sts by inserting the left needle from front to back and purl the stitch twisted (through the back loop). 1 stitch increased.

M1R Make 1 right (right-leaning increase), knit the strand between 2 stitches by inserting the left needle from back to front and knit the stitch (through the front loop). 1 stitch increased.

M1Rp Make 1 right purl (right-leaning increase), purl the strand between 2 stitches by inserting the left needle from back to front and purl the stitch (through the front loop). 1 stitch increased.

P purl

PM place marker

P2tog Purl 2 stitches together. 1 stitch decreased.

P3tog Purl 3 stitches together. 2 stitches decreased.

RC right cross cable

RM remove marker

rnd(s) round(s)

RS right side

sl1 slip 1 stitch (without knitting it) from the left to the right needle

SM slip marker

ssk Slip, slip, knit. Slip the first stitch as if to knit, slip the second stitch as if to knit. Slide both stitches from the right needle back to the left-hand needle. Knit both stitches through the back loops together as if they were 1 stitch. 1 stitch decreased.

sssk Slip, slip, slip, knit. Slip the first stitch as if to knit, slip the second stitch as if to knit, slip the third stitch as if to knit. Slide all 3 stitches from the right needle back to the left-hand needle. Knit 3 stitches through the back loops together as if they were 1 stitch. 2 stitches decreased.

St(s) stitch(es)

Stockintette st Stockinette stitch. Worked flat: RS: knit, WS: purl; in the round: knit all rounds.

tbl Through back loop. Knit or purl a stitch 'twisted': for a knit stitch insert the right needle through the back loop and knit, for a purl stitch insert the right needle into the back leg of the stitch and purl.

yo Yarn over. Bring the working yarn from the back of the work to the front by moving it between the 2 needles and wrap it over the right needle creating a 'hole' in the fabric. Knit the next stitch as usual. 1 stitch increased.

WS wrong side

wyif with yarn in front

wyib with yarn in back

1/1 LC Left cross cable. Transfer 1 stitch onto a DPN or cable needle and keep in front of work, knit 1, then knit 1 from the DPN or cable needle.

1/1 RC Right cross cable. Transfer 1 stitch onto a DPN or cable needle and keep in back of work, knit 1, then knit 1 from the DPN or cable needle.

2/2 LC Left cross cable. Transfer 2 stitches onto a DPN or cable needle and keep in front of work, knit 2, then knit 2 from the DPN or cable needle.

2/2 RC Right cross cable. Transfer 2 stitches onto a DPN or cable needle and keep in back of work, knit 2, then knit 2 from the DPN or cable needle.

3/3 LC Left cross cable. Transfer 3 stitches onto a DPN or cable needle and keep in front of work, knit 3, then knit 3 from the DPN or cable needle.

3/3 RC Right cross cable. Transfer 3 stitches onto a DPN or cable needle and keep in back of work, knit 3, then knit 3 from the DPN or cable needle.

1/1 RPC Right purl cross cable. Transfer 1 stitch onto a DPN and keep in back of work, knit 1, then purl 1 from DPN.

1/1 LPC Left purl cross cable. Transfer 1 stitch onto a DPN and keep in front of work, purl 1, then knit 1 from DPN.

2/1 RPC Right purl cross cable. Transfer 1 stitch onto a DPN and keep in back of work, knit 2, then purl 1 from DPN.

2/1 LPC Left purl cross cable. Transfer 2 stitches onto a DPN and keep in front of work, purl 1, then knit 2 from DPN.

1/1/1 LPC Left purl cross cable. Transfer 2 stitches onto a DPN and keep in front of work, knit 1, transfer the last stitch from DPN (stitch number 2) onto the left needle and purl that stitch, then from the DPN: knit 1.

1/1/2 RPC Right purl cross cable. Transfer 2 stitches onto a DPN and keep in back of work, knit 1, transfer the last stitch from DPN (stitch number 2) onto the left needle and purl that stitch, then from the DPN: knit 1.

1/1/2 LPC Left purl cross cable. Transfer 3 stitches onto a DPN and keep in front of work, knit 1, transfer last stitch from DPN (stitch number 3) onto left needle and purl that stitch, then from the DPN: knit 2.

2/1/2 RPC Right purl cross cable. Transfer 3 stitches onto a DPN and keep in back of work, knit 2, transfer the last stitch from DPN (stitch number 3) onto the left needle and purl that stitch, then from the DPN: knit 2.

2/1/2 LPC Transfer 3 stitches onto a DPN and keep in front of work, knit 2, transfer the last stitch from DPN (stitch number 3) onto the left needle and purl that stitch, then from the DPN: knit 2.

SPECIAL TECHNIQUES

5-st bobble
(used in My Favourite Story sweater pattern)

Create a 5-st bobble into the same stitch as follows: knit 1, yarn over, knit 1, yarn over, knit 1. Do one more yarn over on the right needle, then using the left needle: pull the 1st st on the right needle over the yarn over, pull the 2nd st over the yarn over, pull the 3rd st over the yarn over, pull the 4th st over the yarn over, pull the 5th st over the yarn over. Secure the bobble in place as follows: using the left needle, pick up the strand that is right below the bobble you've just created from the WS side and transfer onto the right needle. Pull the 2nd st on the right needle over the st you just picked up. Bobble is secured and complete.

Tip! *Head to my YouTube channel for a video tutorial on how to create a 5-st bobble, search for the Love Letter Top video tutorial.*

DS = Double stitch
(used in German Short Rows for the Coffee Run sweater pattern)

The double stitch is always worked on the first stitch of the row following a turn. The first stitch on the left needle is slipped purlwise with yarn in front (wyif), then the yarn is pulled tightly over the needle so that the two legs of the stitch in the row below are pulled up and exposed on the right needle. Continue working the row as the pattern says. On the next row, work the double stitch as a 'normal' stitch, either knitting or purling it as normal.

Tip! *Head to my YouTube channel for a video tutorial on how to work German Short Rows, search for the Cinema Sweater video tutorial.*

This raglan sweater offers a modern twist on a romantic classic. Urban Romance is knit from the top down, combining delicate lace on the front and back with cosy honeycomb stitches on the sleeves. It's the perfect mix of soft and sophisticated, effortlessly adding a touch of femininity to your weekend museum trips or park strolls. Whether you're dressing up or down, Urban Romance brings a bit of love to your everyday style.

URBAN ROMANCE

STYLING TIP #1

Ready for party season? Elevate your knit with a festive twist by styling it with a glittery skirt and a chic statement bag for the perfect blend of cosy and glam.

Sizes

XS–S (M–L, XL–2XL) (3XL–4XL, 5XL)

Finished garment measurements

Bust circumference: 98 (111, 124.5) (138, 153.5) cm / 38.5 (43.75, 49) (54.25, 60.5)".

Length from underarm to hem: 29 (29, 33.5) (33.5, 38.5) cm / 11.25 (11.25, 13) (13, 15)".

Sleeve length from underarm: 33.5 cm / 13" all sizes.

Upper sleeve circumference: 48 (54.5, 61) (62, 62) cm / 19 (21.5, 24) (24.5, 24.5)".

Cuff circumference: 16.5 (18.5, 21) (23.5, 23.5) cm / 6.5 (7, 8) (9, 9)".

Choose the size that is 5–15 cm / 2–6" larger than your bust circumference depending on how fitted you prefer the garment.

Sample shown in size XS–S (Kika has a bust of approx. 89 cm / 35").

Gauge

18 sts × 26 rnds = 10 cm / 4" on 5 mm / US 8 needles in lace sample stitch Chart A2, after blocking.

24 sts × 32 rows/rnds = 10 cm / 4" on 3 mm / US 2.5 needles in *k1 tbl, p1*, after blocking.

Needles

3 mm / US 2.5: circular needles 40–60 cm / 16–24" for neck opening and 80–100 cm / 32–40" for hem rib, and DPNs for sleeve rib (or use the Magic Loop technique instead).

5 mm / US 8: circular needles 40–60 cm / 16–24" for the sleeves and 80–100 cm / 32–40" for body, or just 80–100 cm / 32–40" needles if you're using the Magic Loop technique.

Notions

Cable needle, removable (open) stitch markers, tapestry needle, stitch holders or scrap yarn.

Suggested yarn

The sweater is worked with one strand of DK weight yarn held together with one strand of lace weight yarn.

You need approx. 1400 (1540, 1680) (1820, 1960 m / 1531 (1684, 1837) (1990, 2143) yds of DK weight yarn and 1400 (1540, 1680) (1820, 1960) m / 1531 (1684, 1837) (1990, 2143) yds of lace weight yarn.

Sample knitted with yarns

500 (550, 600) (625, 650) Sandnes Garn Double Sunday (100% merino wool – 108 m / 118 yds / 50 g) in the colour Peach 4033 **together with** 155 (170, 185) (200, 220) g of Knitting for Olive Soft Silk Mohair (70% mohair, 30% silk – 225m / 246 yds / 25 g) in the colour Poppy Rose.

The sweater is worked by holding one strand of merino and one strand of silk mohair together.

DIRECTIONS

This raglan sweater is knitted seamlessly from the top down. It has a decorative lace motif that repeats on the front, back and sleeves together with a textured honeycomb stitch. The sleeves are shaped with increases for added volume and finished with twisted rib cuffs for a balloon-shaped silhouette.

Collar

Cast on 96 (96, 96) (96, 112) sts with 3 mm / US 2.5 (40–60 cm / 16–24") circular needles using the Backwards Loop Cast-On method (or your preferred cast-on method).
Note! The cast on edge will be hidden when the collar is folded inside and sewn.

Join to work in the rnd and place a marker to indicate the beginning of rnd (this is BOR-m).

Work *k1 tbl, p1* rib until work measures 10 cm / 4" in total.

Yoke

Change to 5 mm / US 8 (80–100 cm / 32–40") circular needles, and place 7 removable markers for raglan seams as follows (starting from BOR-m):
5 sts (= raglan seam), PM, 11 sts (= sleeve), PM, 5 sts (= raglan seam), PM, 27 (27, 27, 27, 35) (= front), PM, 5 sts (= raglan seam), PM, 11 sts (= sleeve), PM, 5 sts (= raglan seam), PM, 27 (27, 27, 27, 35) (=back).

Begin working the yoke according to the charts as follows:

Rnd 1: K1 tbl, *p1, k1 tbl* to m (= raglan seam), SM, work row 1 of Chart B1 (= sleeve), SM, k1 tbl, *p1, k1 tbl* to m (= raglan seam), SM, work row 1 of Chart A1, work row 3 of Chart A2, work row 1 of A3 (= front), SM, k1 tbl, *p1, k1 tbl* to m (= raglan seam), SM, work row 1 of Chart B1 (= sleeve), SM, k1 tbl, *p1, k1 tbl* to m (= raglan seam), SM, work row 1 of Chart A1, work row 3 of Chart A2, work row 1 of Chart A3 (= back).

Rnd 2: K1 tbl, *p1, k1 tbl* to m, SM, work the next row of Chart B1 (= sleeve), SM, k1 tbl, *p1, k1 tbl* to m, SM, work the next rows of Charts: A1, A2, A3 (= front), SM, k1 tbl, *p1, k1 tbl* to m, SM, work the next row of Chart B1 (= sleeve), SM, k1 tbl, *p1, k1 tbl* to m, SM, work the next row of Charts: A1, A2, A3 (= back).

Rnds 3–26: Continue in this manner, always working the next row of Charts A1, A2, A3 (front and back) and B1 (sleeves) until rows 3–26 are completed once.

Rnd 27: K1 tbl, *p1, k1 tbl* to m, SM, work row 1 of Chart B2 (= sleeve), SM, k1 tbl, *p1, k1 tbl* to m, SM, work row 27 of Chart A1, work row 1 of Chart A2, work row 27 of Chart A3 (= front), SM, k1 tbl, *p1, k1 tbl* to m, SM, work row 1 of Chart B2 (= sleeve), SM, k1 tbl, *p1, k1 tbl* to m, SM, work row 27 of Chart A1, work row 1 of Chart A2, work row 27 of Chart A3 (= back).

Rnds 28-50: Continue in the same manner, always working the next row of each chart until rows 28–50 of Charts A1, A2 and A3 (front and back) are completed once, and rows 1–12 of Chart B2 (sleeves) completed twice.

There are 304 (304, 304) (304, 320) sts in total. Front and back: 77 (77, 77) (77, 85) sts for each Front and Back. Sleeves: 65 (65, 65) (65, 65) sts for each Sleeve. Raglan seams: 5 sts for each raglan seam (4 seams in total).

Size M–L
Rnds 51–62: Continue in the same manner, always working the next row of Charts A1, A2 and A3 (front and back) until rows

51–62 are completed. Work the next row of Chart B2 (sleeves) until rows 1–12 are completed once.

Size XL–2XL
Rnds 51–74: Continue in the same manner, always working the next row of Charts A1, A2 and A3 (front and back) until rows 51–74 are completed. Work the next row of Chart B2 (sleeves) until rows 1–12 are completed twice.

Sizes 3XL–4XL and 5XL
Rnds 51–86: Continue in the same manner, always working the next row of Charts A1, A2 and A3 (front and back) until rows 51–86 are completed. Work the next row of Chart B2 (sleeves) until rows 1–12 are completed three times.

There are 304 (352, (400) (448, 464) sts in total for the yoke. Front and back: 77 (89, 101) (113, 121) sts for each Front and Back. Sleeves: 65 (77, 89) (101, 101) sts for each Sleeve. Raglan seams: 5 sts for each raglan seam (4 seams in total).

Body

Next, the body will be joined in the rnd. Sleeve sts will be placed on hold, and new sts will be cast on for the underarms. The cable and lace charts will be continued as established.

Work as follows:
Transfer 5 raglan sts onto a st holder, RM, transfer 65 (77, 89) (101, 101) sleeve sts onto a st holder, RM, transfer 5 raglan sts onto a st holder, cast on 11 sts for the underarm with the Backwards Loop Cast-On method, work row 1 of Chart C across 77 (89, 101) (113, 121) front sts, SM, transfer 5 raglan sts onto a st holder, RM, transfer 65 (77, 89) (101, 101) sleeve sts onto a st holder, RM, transfer 5 raglan sts onto a st holder, cast on 11 sts for underarm with the Backwards Loop Cast-On method, RM, work row 1 of Chart C across 77 (89, 101) (113, 121) back sts as established. Place a marker to indicate the beginning of rnd (this is BOR-m).

There are 176 (200, 224) (248, 276) sts in total for the body.

Continue working in est pattern for back and front according to Chart C as follows (k all the sts for the underarm on the first rnd instead of doing the 1/1 cables):

Rnd 1: Work row 2 of Chart C to m (= front), SM, work row 2 of Chart C to BOR-m (= back).
Rnd 2: Work the next row of Chart C (= front) to m, SM, work the next row of Chart C (= back) to BOR-m.

Continue working like this (repeating rows 1–2) until all rows 1–12 of Chart C are completed 5 (5) 6 (6) 7 more times (or until work measures 6 cm / 2.25" less than desired total length).

Change to 3 mm / US 2.5 circular needles and work *k1 tbl, p1* rib until the hem measures 6 cm / 2.25" and bind off using the Italian Bind-Off method (or your preferred stretchy bind-off method).

Sleeves

Transfer the first 5 raglan sts, the 65 (77, 89) (101, 101) sleeve sts, and then last 5 raglan sts that were on hold onto 5 mm / US 8 (40–60 cm / 16–24") circular needles.

Beginning from the middle of underarm, pick up and k 6 sts, k1 tbl, [p1, k1 tbl] 2 times, PM, work row 1 of Chart D to last 5 sleeve sts, PM, k1 tbl, [p1, k1 tbl] 2 times, pick up and k 5 sts from underarm. Place a marker to indicate the beginning of rnd (= BOR-m).

There are 86 (98, 110) (112, 112) sts in total for the sleeve (= 21 sts for the ribbed underarm section and 65 (77, 89) (101, 101) sts for the charted section between the two markers).

Rnd 1: K1 tbl, *p1, k1 tbl* to m, SM, work row 2 of Chart D to m, SM, *k1 tbl, p1* to the end of rnd.

Rnd 2: K1 tbl, *p1, k1 tbl* to m, SM, work the next row of Chart D to m, SM, *k1 tbl, p1* to the end of rnd.

Continue working like this repeating rnd 2 until rows 1–12 of Chart D are completed three times.

Then work one rnd of increases as follows:
Rnd 1 (inc rnd 1): [K1, yo, k1] into the same st, *p1, k1 tbl* to m, SM, work rnd 1 of Chart D to m, SM, *k1 tbl, p1* to end of rnd. 2 sts increased.

There are 88 (100, 112) (124, 124) sts in total for the sleeve.

Rnd 2: K1 tbl, *p1, k1 tbl* to m, SM, work the next rnd of Chart D to m, SM, *k1 tbl, p1* to end of rnd.

Continue working like this repeating rnd 2 until row 1–12 of Chart D are completed once.

Work one more rnd of increases as follows:
Rnd 1 (inc rnd 2): [K1, yo, k1] into the same st, *p1, k1 tbl* to m, SM, work row 1 of Chart D to m, SM, *k1 tbl, p1* to end of rnd. 2 sts increased.

There are 90 (102, 114) (126, 126) sts in total for the sleeve.

Rnd 2: K1 tbl, *p1, k1 tbl* to m, SM, work the next row of Chart D to m, SM, *k1 tbl, p1* to end of rnd.
Continue repeating rnd 2 until rows 1–12 of Chart D are completed once.

Then continue as established until all rows 1–12 of Chart D are completed once more.

Work one set-up rnd before working the sleeve cuff:
K1, p1, *k2tog, p2tog* to end of rnd.

There are 46 (52, 58)(64, 64) sleeve sts in total.

Change to 3 mm / US 2.5 circular needles and work *k1 tbl, p1* rib until the cuff rib measures 6 cm / 2.5" and bind off using the Italian Bind-Off method.

Work the other sleeve the same.

Finishing

Fold the collar double and attach it by hand sewing loosely on the inside to prevent the neckline from becoming too tight. Weave in all loose ends.

CHART A2

19	18	17	16	15	14	13	12	11	10	9	8	7	6	5	4	3	2	1	
•	Q	•	\	O		O	/	•	Q	•	\	O		O	/	•	Q	•	4
•	Q	•						•	Q	•						•	Q	•	3
•	Q	•						•	Q	•						•	Q	•	2
•	Q	•						•	Q	•						•	Q	•	1

When working across each row of the chart, work the Pattern Repeat section 2 (2, 2) (2, 3) times.

- (blank) knit
- • purl
- O yo
- / knit 3 together
- \ slip, slip, slip, knit
- Q knit through back loop
- (orange box) pattern repeat
- (purple box) pattern repeat

CHART A1 PART 2

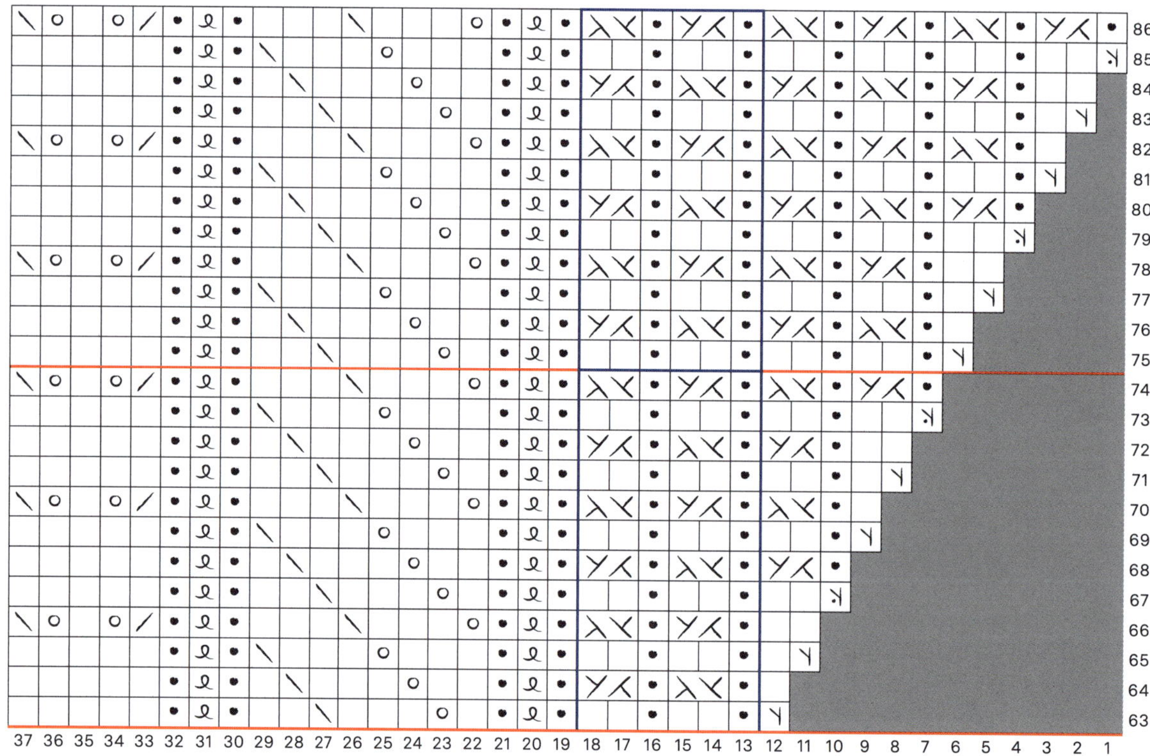

CHART A1 PART 1

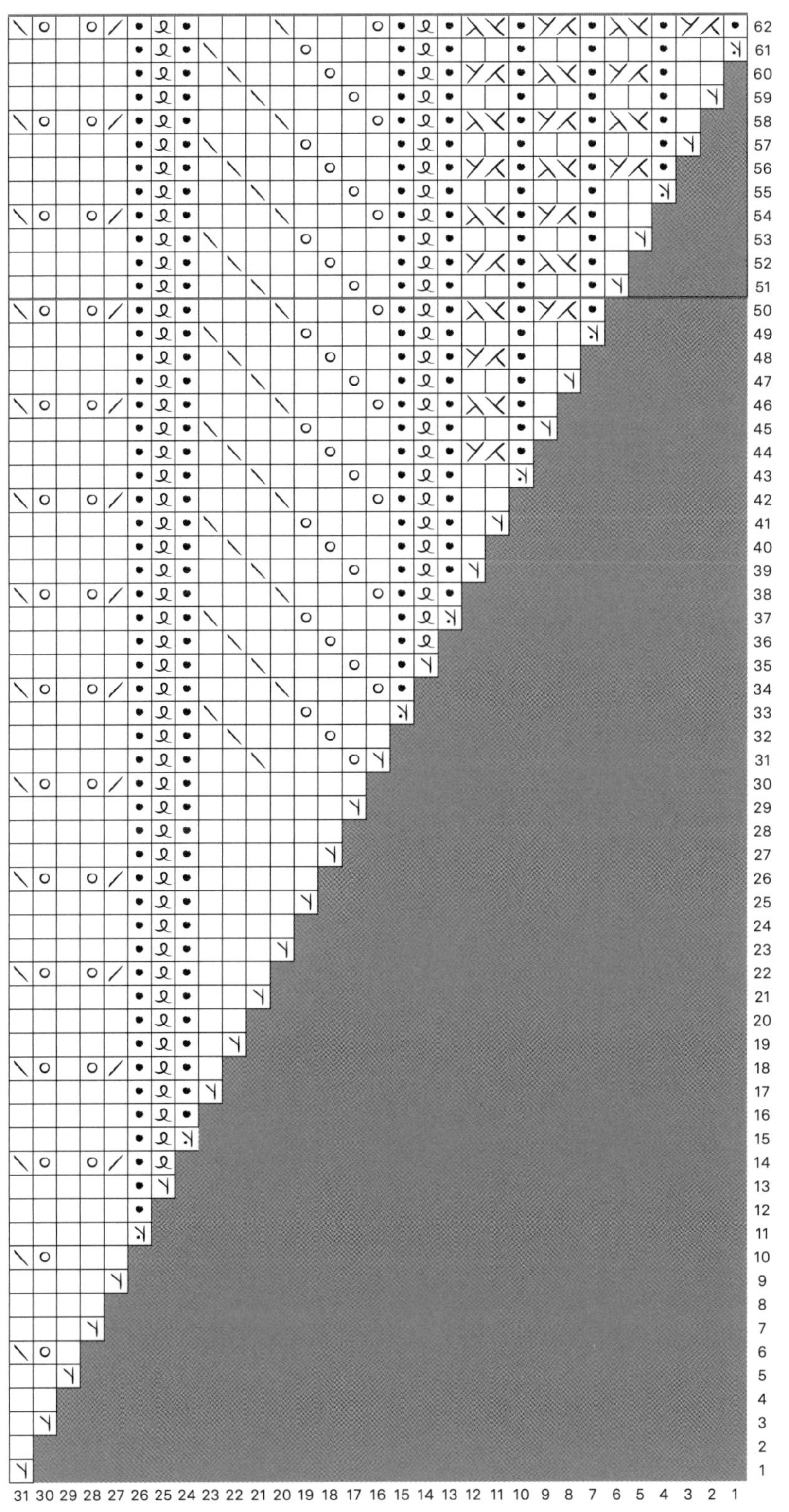

knit

purl

yo

knit 3 together

slip, slip, slip, knit

knit through back loop

1/1 LC

1/1 RC

m1l

m1r

m1lp

m1rp

no stitch

CHART A3 PART 1

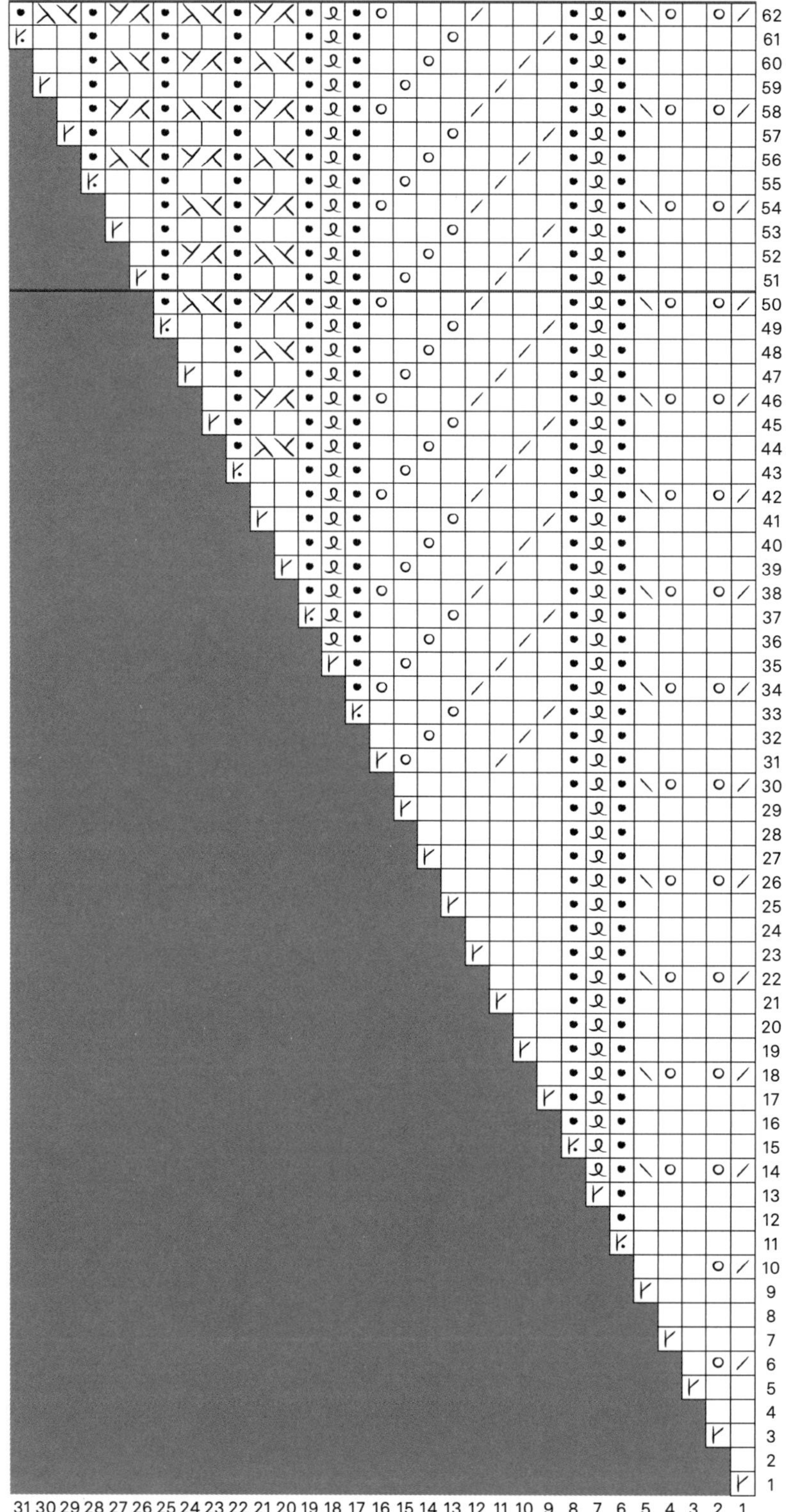

CHART A3 PART 2

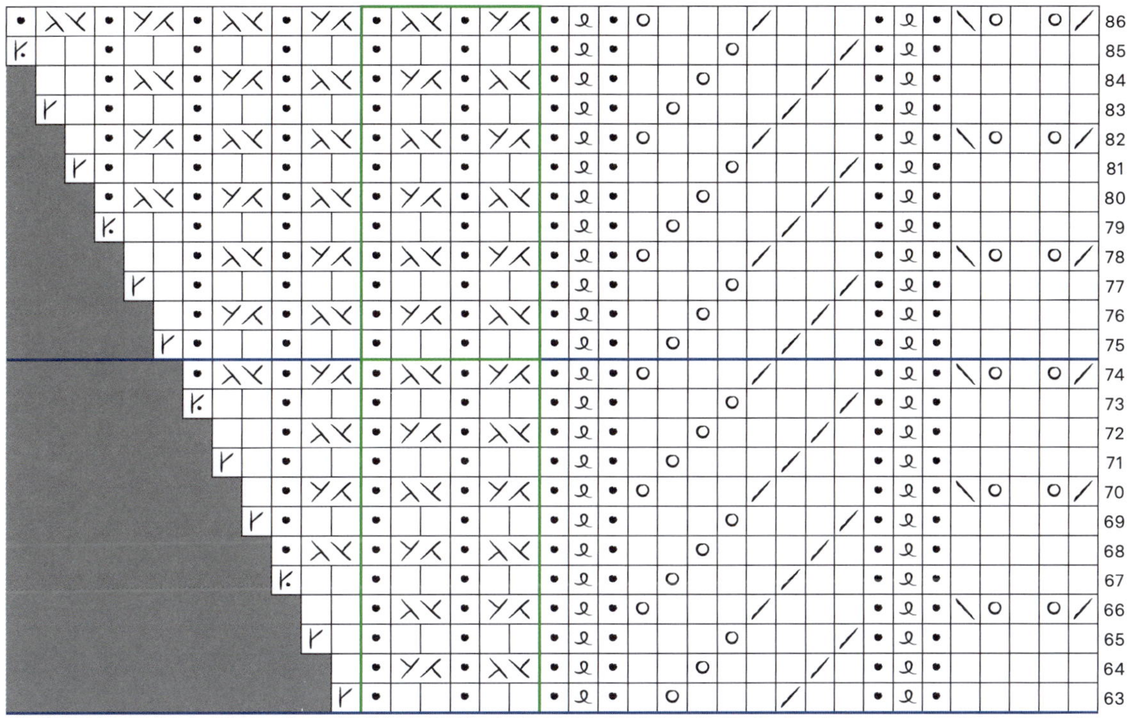

- knit
- purl
- yo
- knit 3 together
- slip, slip, slip, knit
- knit through back loop
- 1/1 LC
- 1/1 RC
- m1l
- m1r
- m1lp
- m1rp
- no stitch
- pattern repeat
- pattern repeat

CHART B1

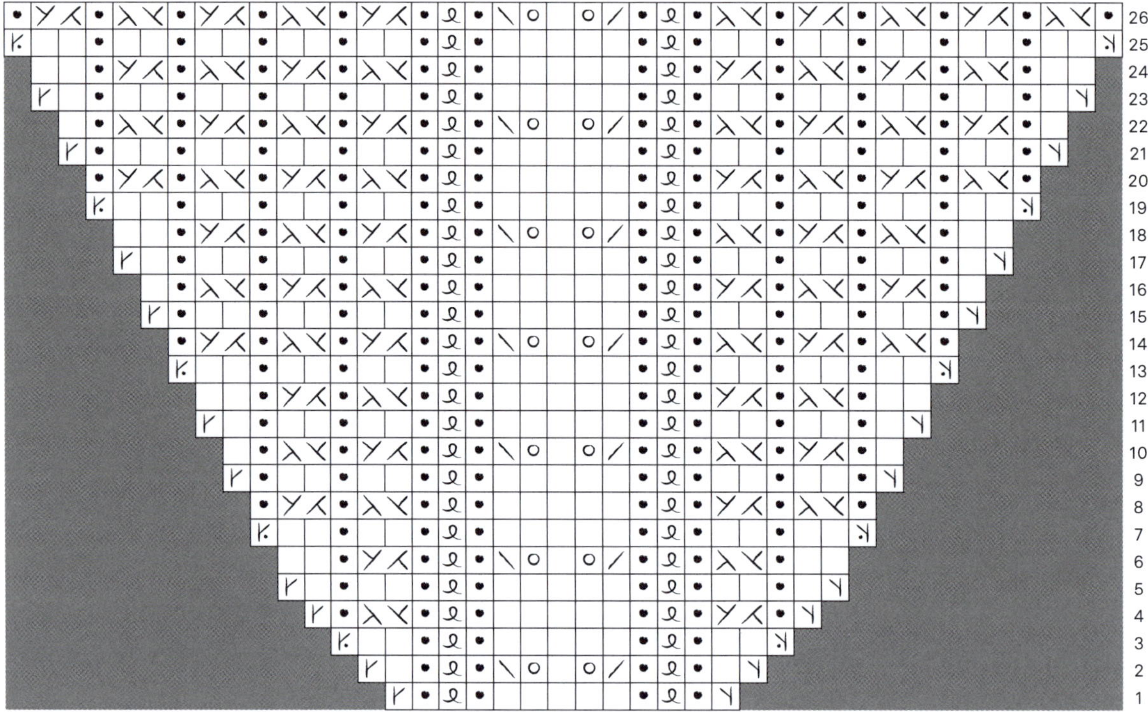

CHART B2

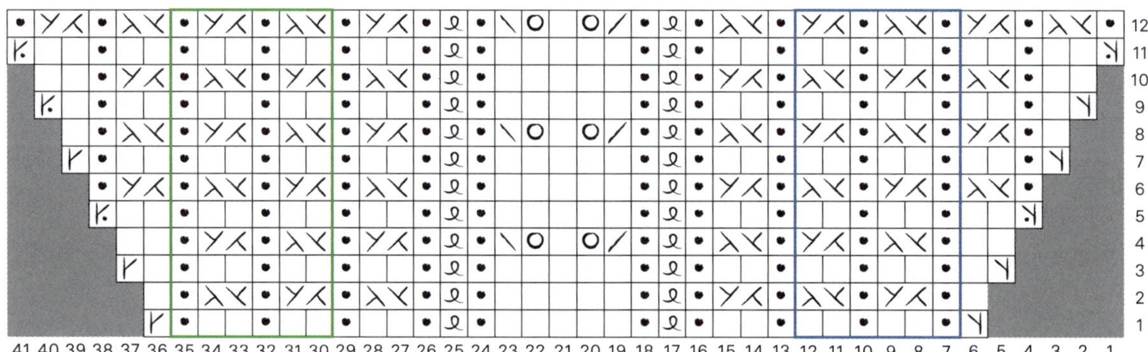

Each time all rows 1–12 of Chart B2 are completed once, the amount of times to work the pattern repeats (columns 7–12 and 30–35) increase by 1.

CHART C

When working across each row of the chart, work the Pattern Repeat sections as follows: Work Pattern Repeat C1: 1 (2, 3) (4, 4) times, Repeat C2: 3 (3, 3) (3, 4) times, and Repeat C3: 1 (2, 3) (4, 4) times.

CHART D

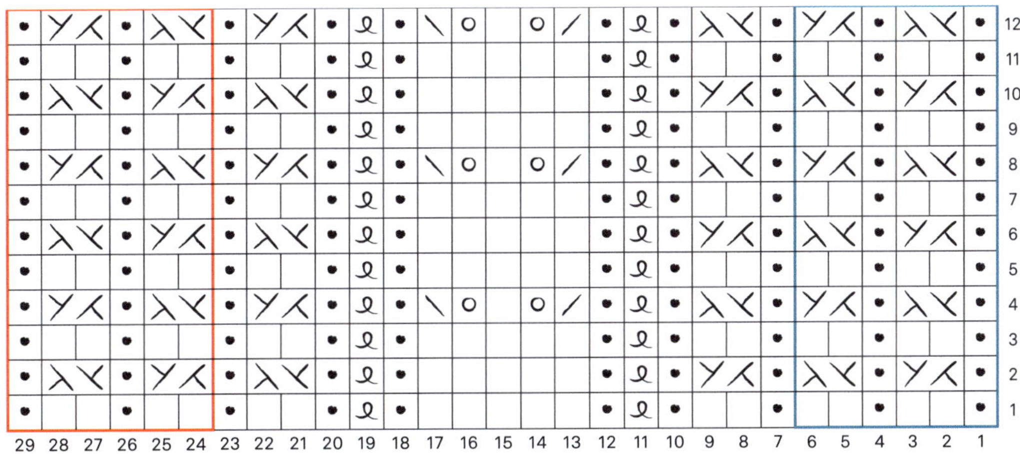

When working across each row of the chart, work the Pattern Repeat sections as follows: Work Pattern Repeat D1: 4 (5, 6) (7, 7) times, work and Repeat D2: 4 (5, 6) (7, 7) times.

- knit
- purl
- yo
- knit 3 together
- slip, slip, slip, knit
- knit through back loop
- 1/1 LC
- 1/1 RC
- m1l
- m1r
- m1lp
- m1rp
- no stitch
- pattern repeat C1
- pattern repeat C2
- pattern repeat C3
- pattern repeat D1
- pattern repeat D2
- pattern repeat
- pattern repeat

When this sweater enters your closet, you'll probably want to pull it out and wear it all the time! The relaxed and oversized fit makes Simple Things an uncomplicated and easy garment for many occasions. Style it with jeans for a casual look, tailored trousers for the office, or a floral or sparkly skirt for brunch with a friend. Its simple design ensures it will become a classic in your handmade wardrobe, worn again and again.

SIMPLE THINGS

STYLING TIP #2

Pair an oversized sweater with a flowy dress and a statement necklace for a casual look that exudes boho chic, blending comfort with a touch of playful style.

STYLING TIP #3

The secret to mastering the 'effortlessly chic' look lies in simplicity and carefully curating each element of your outfit. Opt for well-cut pieces made from high-quality materials: think a classic knit with your favourite jeans, a sleek bag, and a few delicate jewellery pieces to create a minimal yet sophisticated vibe.

Sizes

XXS (XS, S, M) (L, XL, 2XL) (3XL, 4XL, 5XL)

Finished garment measurements

Bust circumference: 107.5 (118, 128.5, 139) (151.5, 160, 170.5) (181, 189.5, 200) cm / 42.25 (46.5, 50.5, 54.75) (59.75, 63, 67.25) (71.25, 74.5, 78.75)".

Body length from underarm: 42 (43, 44, 45) (46, 46, 47) (47, 48, 48) cm / 16.5 (17, 17.25, 17.75) (18, 18, 18.5) (18.5, 19, 19)".

Sleeve length from underarm: 40 (41, 42, 42) (42, 43, 43) (43, 44, 44) cm / 15.75 (16.25, 16.5, 16.5) (16.5, 17, 17) (17, 17.25, 17.25)".

Upper sleeve circumference: 37 (40, 42, 44) (47.5, 47.5, 49.5) (49.5, 51.5, 53.5) cm / 14.5 (15.75, 16.5, 17.25) (18.75, 18.75, 19.5) (19.5, 20.25, 21)".

The Simple Things sweater is designed to have a generous amount of ease. Choose a size that is 30–40 cm / 11.75–15.75" bigger than your bust circumference for a relaxed and oversized look.

Sample shown in size M, Kika has a bust of approx. 89 cm / 35".

Gauge

19 sts × 26 rows/rnds = 10 cm / 4" in Stockinette st on 4.5 mm / US 7 needles, after blocking.

25 sts × 32 rows/rnds = 10 cm / 4" in *k1 tbl, p1* on 3 mm / US 2.5 needles, after blocking.

Needles

3 mm / US 2.5: circular needles 40–60 cm / 16–24" for neck opening and 80–100 cm / 32–40" for hem rib, and DPNs for sleeve rib (or use the Magic Loop technique instead).
4.5 mm/ US7: circular needles 40–60 cm / 16–24" for sleeves and 80–100 cm / 32–40" for body, or just 80-100 cm /32–40" needles if you're using the Magic Loop technique.

Notions

Removable stitch markers, tapestry needle, stitch holder or scrap yarn.

Suggested yarn

The Simple Things sweater can be worked with one strand of DK weight yarn or by holding two strands of fingering weight together.

You need approx. 1250 (1375, 1500, 1563) (1625, 1688, 1750) (1813, 1875, 1938) m / 1367 (1504, 1640, 1709) (1777, 1846, 1914) (1983, 2051, 2120) yds of DK weight yarn or 2500 (2750, 3000, 3125) (3250, 3375, 3500) (3625, 3750, 3875) m / 2734 (3007, 3281, 3414) (3548, 3682, 3815) (3949, 4082, 4216) yds of fingering weight yarn held double.

Samples knitted with yarns

Cream coloured sample: 500 (550, 600, 625) (650, 675, 700) (725, 750, 775) g of Knitting for Olive Merino (100% merino wool – 250 m / 273 yds / 50 g) in the colour Cream.

Sample worked by holding two strands of merino together.

Pink sample: 500 (550, 600, 625) (650, 675, 700) (725, 750, 775) g of John Arbon Textiles Knit by Numbers DK (50% Bluefaced Leicester, 50% Falklands Merino – 250 m / 274 yds / 100 g) in colour 24 **together with** 150 (170, 185, 190) (200, 205, 215) (220, 230, 235) g of Filcolana Tilia (70% kid mohair, 30% silk – 210 m / 230 yds / 25 g) in the colour 370 Flamingo.

Sample worked with one strand of DK merino together with one strand of silk mohair.

DIRECTIONS

The sweater is worked top down seamlessly in Stockinette stitch. The hem and cuffs are finished with a wide rib and the sweater has a soft round neckline shaping with a double-folded collar that gives the sweater a modern and put-together look.

Upper Back

The Upper Back is worked flat. On the first row, removable stitch markers are placed on either side of the neckline to mark where sts will be picked up for the Upper Left and Right Front later.

Cast on 96 (104, 114, 124) (134, 142, 152) (162, 170, 180) sts using the Backwards-Loop Cast-On method (or your preferred cast-on method) with 4.5 mm / US 7 circular needles.

Work as follows:
Row 1 (RS): K29 (32, 35, 39) (44, 48, 52) (57, 61, 66) (= shoulder sts), place a removable marker around the strand between the sts, k 38 (40, 44, 46) (46, 46, 48) (48, 48, 48) (= back neck sts), place a removable marker around the strand between the sts, k all remaining 29 (32, 35, 39) (44, 48, 52) (57, 61, 66) (= shoulder sts).

Row 2 (WS): P to end.

Continue working in Stockinette st until work measures 17 (18, 19, 20) (21, 21, 22) (22, 23, 24) cm / 6.75 (7, 7.5, 8) (8.25, 8.25, 8.75) (8.75, 9, 9.5)" in total from cast-on edge.

Cut the yarn and leave the Upper Back sts to rest while working the Upper Front next.

Left Upper Front

Pick up and k29 (32, 35, 39) (44, 48, 52) (57, 61, 66) sts from the left side stitch marker to the outer edge (when looking at the piece with the RS facing you and the cast-on edge facing up towards the top) with 4.5 mm / US 7 needles, you can remove this marker now.

Work in Stockinette st flat until the Left Upper Front measures 5 (6, 6, 7) (7, 7, 8) (8, 8, 8) cm / 2 (2.25, 2.25, 2.75) (2.75, 2.75, 3.25) (3.25, 3.25, 3.25)" in total from the pick-up edge. End ona WS row.

Start shaping the neckline by working increases next as follows:

Row 1 (RS): K2, M1L, k to end. 1 st increased.
Row 2 (WS): P to end.

Repeat Rows 1–2 ten more times.

There are 40 (43, 46, 50) (55, 59, 63) (68, 72, 77) sts in total.

Cut the yarn and leave the sts to rest as you work the Right Upper Front next.

Right Upper Front

Pick up and k29 (32, 35, 39) (44, 48, 52) (57, 61, 66) sts from the right outer edge to the right side stitch marker (when looking at the piece with the RS facing you and the cast-on edge facing up towards the top) with 4.5 mm / US 7 needles, you can remove this marker now. Work in Stockinette st flat until the Right Upper Front measures 5 (6, 6, 7) (7, 7, 8) (8, 8, 8) cm / 2 (2.25, 2.25, 2.75) (2.75, 2.75, 3.25) (3.25, 3.25, 3.25)" in total from the pick-up edge. End on a WS row.

Start shaping the neckline by working increases next as follows:
Row 1 (RS): K to last 2 sts, M1R, k2. 1 st increased.
Row 2 (WS): P to end.

Repeat Rows 1–2 ten more times.

There are 40 (43, 46, 50) (55, 59, 63) (68, 72, 77) sts in total.

Don't cut the yarn.

Joining the Left and Right Upper Front

Next, connect the Left and Right Upper Fronts to form the Upper Front and cast on new sts to form the middle of the neckline.

Work as follows:
Row 1 (RS): K to end of the right front sts, cast on 16 (18, 22, 24) (24, 24, 26) (26, 26, 26) sts with the Backwards Loop Cast-On method, connect the Left Upper Front sts that were on hold and k to end.

There are 96 (104, 114, 124) (134, 142, 152) (162, 170, 180) sts.

Continue working in Stockinette st flat until The Upper Front measures 17 (18, 19, 20) (21, 21, 22) (22, 23, 24) cm / 6.75 (7, 7.5, 8) (8.25, 8.25, 8.75) (8.75, 9, 9.5)" in total from the pick-up edge. End on a WS row.

Don't cut the yarn.

Body

Next join the Upper Front and Upper Back to form the body on 4.5 mm / US 7 (80–100 cm / 32–40") circular needles and start working in the rnd as follows:

K across the 96 (104, 114, 124) (134, 142, 152) (162, 170, 180) sts for the front, cast on 6 (8, 8, 8) (10, 10, 10) (10, 10, 10) sts with the Backwards Loop Cast-On method for the underarm, k across the 96 (104, 114, 124) (134, 142, 152) (162, 170, 180) sts for the back, cast on 6 (8, 8, 8) (10, 10, 10) (10, 10, 10) sts with the Backwards Loop Cast-On method for the underarm, place beginning of rnd marker.

There are 204 (224, 244, 264) (288, 304, 324) (344, 360, 380) sts.

Work in Stockinette st in the rnd until the body measures 30 (31, 32, 33) (34, 34, 35) (35, 36, 36) cm / 11.75 (12.25, 12.5, 13.3) (13.5, 13.5, 13.75) (13.75, 14.25, 14.25)" from underarm (or, until the body measures 12 cm/ 4.75" less than total desired length).

Change to 3 mm / US 2.5 circular needles and work *k1 tbl, p1* ribbing until the hem measures 12 cm / 4.75" in total. Bind off all sts using the Italian Bind-Off method (or your preferred stretchy bind-off method).

Sleeves

For the sleeves, sts are picked up and knitted along the armhole openings. The sleeves are worked in the rnd in Stockinette st on either 4.5 mm / US 7 (40–60 cm / 16–24") circular needles, DPNs or longer circular needles for the Magic Loop technique.

With the RS facing, pick up and k 70 (76, 80, 84) (90, 90, 94) (94, 98, 102) sts evenly around the armhole opening starting from the middle of the underarm, the rhythm for picking up sts is approx. 3 sts per 4 sts/rows. Join in the rnd and place a marker to mark the beginning of rnd.

Work in Stockinette st in the rnd until the sleeve measures 28 (29, 30, 30) (30, 31, 31) (31, 32, 32) cm / 11 (11.5, 11.75, 12) (11.75, 12.25, 12.25) (12.25, 12.5, 12.5)" from underarm (or, until the sleeve measures 12 cm / 4.75" less than total desired length).

Change to 3 mm / US 2.5 DPNs or circular needles (the Magic Loop technique) and work *k1 tbl, p1* ribbing until the cuff measures 12 cm / 4.75". Bind off all sts using the Italian Bind-Off method.

Work the other sleeve the same way.

Collar

For the collar, sts are picked up along the neckline edge and worked in a twisted rib.

With 3 mm / US 2.5 needles, starting at the right shoulder seam (when looking at the sweater from the back with the RS facing you), pick up and k 94 (102, 114, 118) (118, 120, 122) (126, 126, 126) sts in total from around the neckline as follows:

Pick up and k 38 (40, 44, 46) (46, 46, 48) (48, 48, 48) sts from the back cast-on neckline (k1 in every st), pick up and k 20 (22, 24, 24) (24, 24, 24) (26, 26, 26) sts from the curved edge, pick up and k 16 (18, 22, 24) (24, 24, 26) (26, 26, 26) from the middle front neckline (k1 in every st), pick up and k 20 (22, 24, 24) (24, 24, 24) (26, 26, 26) sts from the curved edge. Place BOR-m.

Work *k1 tbl, p1* ribbing in the rnd until the collar measures 11 cm / 4.25" in total.

Bind off using the Standard Bind-Off method loosely (or your preferred stretchy bind-off method, the edge will be hidden when the collar is folded and sewn on the inside).

Finishing

Fold the collar double and attach on the inside by sewing it loosely to the pick-up edge. Weave in all ends.

A casual, minimalist everyday accessory that effortlessly combines comfort and style, Keep It Together is a versatile beanie that is worked from the bottom up. It allows you to easily adjust the length to suit your personal preferences, ensuring an ideal fit. It features a double-folded brim that pulls it all together for a street-smart look. The unisex design makes it easy to wear with many different styles.

KEEP IT TOGETHER

STYLING TIP #4
Spice it up by transforming a simple denim outfit with a vibrant pop of colour.

Sizes

One size.

Finished garment measurements

Brim circumference: 38 cm / 15".
Height when fold is open: 34.5 cm / 13.5".
Height with brim folded: 23.5 cm / 9.25".

The beanie is designed to have about 12–17 cm / 4.75–6.75" of negative ease as the fabric will stretch out quite a bit when worn.

Gauge

25 sts × 29 rnds = 10 cm / 4" on 3 mm / US 2.5 needles in 2 × 2 rib, after blocking when the fabric is relaxed and not stretched out.

Needles

3 mm / US 2.5: circular needles 40–60 cm / 16–24" (or longer ones for the Magic Loop technique), and 3 mm / US 2.5: DPNs for crown shaping if you're not using the Magic Loop technique.

Notions

Stitch markers, tapestry needle.

Suggested yarn

The beanie is worked with one strand of DK weight yarn or two strands of fingering weight yarn held together.

You need approx. 500 m / 547 yds of fingering weigh yarn or 250 m / 273 yds of DK weight yarn.

Sample knitted with yarn

100 g of Knitting for Olive Merino (100% merino wool – 250 m / 273 yds / 50 g) in the colour Pomegranate. The beanie is worked by holding two strands of merino together.

DIRECTIONS

The beanie is worked in a 2 × 2 rib in the round. The beanie is worked bottom up and the length can be customised to fit your preferences exactly. The brim is folded twice at the end.

Brim

Cast on 96 sts with the Long-Tail Cast-On method for 2 × 2 rib with 3 mm / US 2.5 circular needles. Join in the rnd and place BOR–m.

Work *k2, p2* rib until the beanie measures 6 cm / 2.5" in total.

First fold: Work one rnd of k sts. This will create a rnd of p sts on the outside which will help the fold to stay in place neatly.

Second fold: Work *k2, p2* rib until the beanie measures 6.5 cm / 2.75" from the rnd of k sts (or, until the beanie measures 12.5 cm / 5.25" in total). Work one more rnd of k sts for the second fold.

Beanie

Work in *k2, p2* rib until the beanie measures 17 cm / 6.75" from the second rnd of k sts or until the beanie measures 29 cm / 12" in total from the cast-on edge (or until the beanie measures approx. 6.5 cm / 2.75" less that total desired length).

Shaping the crown

Place 4 additional stitch markers on the next rnd as follows (you'll have 5 markers is total after this, including the BOR-m.):

K2, p2 3 times, k1, PM, k1, p2, *k2, p2* 5 times, k1, PM, k1, p2, *k2, p2* 5 times, k1, PM, k1, p2, *k2, p2* 5 times, k1, PM, k1, p2, *k2, p2* 2 times.

You might want to change to 3 mm / US 2.5 DPNs to shape the crown of the beanie if you're not using the Magic Loop technique here.

Rnd 1 (dec rnd): *K2, p2* 2 times, k2, p1, k2tog, [SM, ssk, p1, *k2, p2* 4 times, k2, p1, k2tog] 3 times, SM, ssk, p1, *k2, p2* 2 times. 8 sts decreased.

There are 88 sts in total.

Rnd 2: *K2, p2* 2 times, k2, p1, k1, [SM, k1, p1, *k2, p2* 4 times, k2, p1, k1] 3 times, SM, k1, p1, *k2, p2* 2 times.

Rnd 3 (dec rnd): *K2, p2* 2 times, k2, k2tog, [SM, ssk, *k2, p2* 4 times, k2, k2tog] 3 times, SM, ssk, *k2, p2* 2 times. 8 sts decreased.

There are 80 sts in total.

Rnd 4: *K2, p2* 2 times, k3, [SM, k3, *p2, k2* 3 times, p2, k3] 3 times, SM, k3, p2, k2, p2.

Rnd 5 (dec rnd): *K2, p2* 2 times, k1, k2tog, [SM, ssk, k1, p2, *k2, p2* 3 times, k1, k2tog], SM, ssk, k1, p2, k2, p2. 8 sts decreased.

There are 72 sts in total.

Rnd 6: K2, *p2, k2* 2 times, [SM, K2, *p2, k2* 4 times] 3 times, SM, *k2, p2* 2 times.

Rnd 7 (dec rnd): *K2, p2* 2 times, k2tog, [SM, ssk, p2, *k2, p2* 3 times, k2tog] 3 times, SM, ssk, p2, k2, p2. 8 sts decreased.

There are 64 sts in total.

Rnd 8: *K2, p2* 2 times, k1, [SM, k1, p2, *k2, p2* 3 times, k1] 3 times, SM, k1, p2, k2, p2.

Rnd 9 (dec rnd): K2, *p2, k2* 2 times, p1, k2tog, [SM, ssk, p1, k2, *p2, k2* 2 times, p1, k2tog] 3 times, SM, ssk, p1, k2, p2. 8 sts decreased.

There are 56 sts in total.

Rnd 10: K2, p2, k2, p1, k1, [SM, k1, p1, k2, *p2, k2* 2 times, p1, k1] 3 times, SM, k1, p1, k2, p2.

Rnd 11 (dec rnd): K2, p2, k2, k2tog, [SM, ssk, k2, *p2, k2* 2 times, k2tog] 3 times, SM, ssk, k2, p2. 8 sts decreased.

There are 48 sts in total.

Rnd 12: K2, p2, k3, [SM, k3, p2, k2, p2, k3] 3 times, SM, k3, p2.

Rnd 13 (dec rnd): K2, p2, k1, k2tog, [SM, ssk, k1, p2, k2, p2, k1, k2tog] 3 times, SM, ssk, k1, p2. 8 sts decreased.

There are 40 sts in total.

Rnd 14: K2, p2, k2, [SM, k2, *p2, k2* 2 times] 3 times, SM, k2, p2.

Rnd 15 (dec rnd): K2, p2, k2tog, [SM, ssk, p2, k2, p2, k2tog] 3 times, SM, ssk, p2. 8 sts decreased.

There are 32 sts in total.

Rnd 16: Work *k2, p2* rib across all sts and remove all markers.

Cut the yarn and pull it through all the live sts using a tapestry needle. Pull the yarn tightly so that the crown opening shuts close.

Finishing

Weave in all ends and fold up the brim double.

A true modern classic, this sweater features gorgeous cables decorating the front, back and sleeves. My Favourite Story is worked seamlessly from the top down and its intricate textures make this sweater a show-stopper. The wide, extra-long sleeves add a contemporary touch. You can also choose to work them shorter or style them by folding them to add interesting details to your outfit. The twisted rib at the hem and cuffs gives the garment a polished look.

MY FAVOURITE STORY

STYLING TIP #5

Balance your oversized knit with something form-fitting or reveal a hint of skin to keep the look sleek and avoid getting lost in all that volume.

Sizes

XS (S, M, L) (XL, 2XL) (3XL, 4XL)

Finished garment measurements

Bust circumference: 106 (110, 114, 122) (128, 134) (138, 146) cm / 41.5 (43.5, 45, 48) (50.5, 53) (54.5, 57.5)".

Length from underarm to hem:
28 (37, 45.5, 44) (42.5, 51) (49.5, 58) cm / 11 (14.5, 18, 17.25) (16.75, 20) (19.5, 23)".

Sleeve length from underarm:
38 (37, 35.5, 44) (42.5, 41) (49.5, 48) cm / 15 (14.5, 14, 17.25) (16.75, 16) (19.5, 19)".

Upper sleeve circumference:
33.5 (35.5, 37.5, 41.5) (44.5, 47.5) (50.5, 53.5) cm / 13 (14, 15, 16.5) (17.5, 18.5) (20, 21)".

Choose the size that is 0–15 cm / 0–6" bigger than your bust circumference depending on how loose or tight fitting you prefer the garment to be.

Light blush sample shown in size M (Kika has a bust of approx. 89 cm / 35"), and sage green sample in size L (Juki has a bust of approx. 115 cm / 45").

Gauge

20 sts × 26 rnds = 10 cm / 4" on 5 mm / US 8 needles in sample stitch pattern (after blocking).

Sample stitch

Rnd 1: P to end.
Rnd 2: *K1, p1* to end.

Repeat rnds 1–2.

Needles

3.5 mm / US 4: circular needles 40–60 cm / 16–24" for neck opening and 80–100 cm / 32–40" for hem rib, and DPNs for sleeve rib (or use the Magic Loop technique instead).

5 mm / US 8: circular needles 40–60 cm / 16–24" for the sleeves and 80–100 cm / 32–40" for body, or just 80–100 cm / 32–40" needles if you're using the Magic Loop technique.

Notions

Cable needle, removable (open) stitch markers, tapestry needle, stitch holders or scrap yarn.

Suggested yarn

The sweater is worked by holding two strands of fingering weight yarn together with one strand of lace weight yarn.

You need approx. 2375 (2500, 2625, 2750) (2875, 3000) (3125, 3250) m / 2596 (2734, 2872, 3010) (3149, 3287) (3425, 3563) yds of fingering weight yarn and 1200 (1250, 1315, 1375) (1450, 1500) (1565, 1625) m / 1312 (1367, 1438, 1504) (1586, 1640) (1711, 1778) yds of lace weight yarn.

Samples knitted with yarns

Light blush sample: 600 (625, 675, 700) (725, 750) (775, 825) g Novita Soft Merino 4PLY (100% wool – 200 m / 218 yds / 50 g) in colour 157 **together with** 130 (140, 145, 155) (160, 165) (175, 180) g of Knitting for Olive Soft Silk Mohair (70% mohair, 30% silk – 225m / 246 yds / 25 g) in the colour Cloud.

Sage green sample: 475 (500, 525, 550) (575, 600) (625, 650) g Knitting for Olive Merino (100% merino wool – 250 m / 273 yds / 50 g) in colour Dusty Aqua **together with**

100 (110, 115, 120) (125, 130) (135, 140) g Krea Deluxe Silk Mohair (45% silk, 33% mohair, 22% baby alpaca – 240 m / 262 yds/ 20 g) in the colour 33.

The sweater is worked by holding two strands of merino and one strand of silk mohair together.

DIRECTIONS

The sweater is worked seamlessly from the top down. The sleeves are wide and extra long, you can choose to work them shorter or style them by folding them. The collar is worked double, and folded in half and attached on the inside by hand sewing, or you can choose to leave it as is and fold it outwards for a roll neck instead. The hem and sleeve cuffs are finished with twisted rib.

Collar

Cast on 102 sts on 3.5 mm / US 4 40–60 cm / 16–24" circular needles using the Backwards Loop Cast-On method. **Note!** The cast on edge will be hidden when the collar is folded inside and sewn.

Join to work in rnd and place a marker to indicate the beginning of rnd (= BOR-m).

Work *k1 tbl, p1* ribbing until work measures 10 cm / 4" in total.

Yoke

Change to 5 mm / US 8 80–100 cm / 32–40" circular needles before continuing and place 7 removable markers for raglan seams as follows (starting from BOR-m):
29 sts (= back), PM, 8 sts (= raglan seam), PM, 6 sts (= sleeve), PM, 8 sts (= raglan seam), PM, 29 sts (= front), PM, 8 sts (= raglan seam), PM, 6 sts (= sleeve), PM, 8 sts (= raglan seam).

Start working the yoke according to the charts as follows:

Rnd 1: Work rnd 1 of Chart A (= back), SM, work rnd 1 of Chart B1 (= raglan seam), SM, work rnd 1 of Chart C (= sleeve), SM, work rnd 1 of Chart B1 (= raglan seam), SM, work rnd 1 of Chart A (= front), SM, work rnd 1 of Chart B1 (= raglan seam), SM, work rnd 1 of Chart C (= sleeve), SM, work rnd 1 of Chart B1 (= raglan seam).

Continue in this manner, always working the following rnd of Chart A, B1 and C until all rnds 1–52 are completed.

There are 310 sts in total.

Only sizes S–4XL
Continue working the yoke according to Chart F for the Front and Back and Chart B2 for the raglan seams as follows:

Rnd 1: Work rnd 53 of Chart F (= back), SM, work rnd 53 of Chart B2 (= raglan seam), SM, work rnd 53 of Chart F (= sleeve), SM, work rnd 53 of Chart B2 (= raglan seam), SM, work rnd 53 of Chart F (= front), SM, work rnd 53 of Chart B2 (= raglan seam), SM, work rnd 53 of Chart F (= sleeve), SM, work rnd 53 of Chart B2 (= raglan seam).

Rnd 2: Work the next rnd of Chart F (= back), SM, work the next rnd of Chart B2 (= raglan seam), SM, work the next rnd of Chart F (= sleeve), SM, work the next rnd of Chart B2 (= raglan seam), SM, work the next rnd of Chart F (= front), SM, work the next rnd of Chart B2 (= raglan seam), SM, work the next rnd of Chart F (= sleeve), SM, work the next rnd of Chart B2 (= raglan seam).

Only sizes M–4XL
Continue in this manner, always working the following rnd of Chart F and Chart B2 until rnds – (–, 53–58, 53–62) (53–66, 53–70) (53–74, 53–78) are completed.

There are 310 (318, 334, 350) (366, 382) (398, 414) sts in total. Front and Back: 81 (83, 87, 91) (95, 99) (103, 107) sts for each. Sleeves: 58 (60, 64, 68) (72, 76) (80, 84) sts each. Raglan seams: 8 sts for each raglan seam (4 seams in total).

Body

Next, we're going to knit the body and put the sts for the sleeves on hold.

On the next rnd, work rnd 53 (55, 59, 63) (67, 71) (75, 53) of Chart D (= back) to m, SM, work rnd 1 of Chart B1 to m, RM, transfer 58 (60, 64, 68) (72, 76) (80, 84) sleeve sts onto a holder (for example a stitch wire or just a long piece of yarn), cast on 9 (11, 11, 15) (17, 19) (21, 23) sts for underarm with the Backwards Loop Cast-On method, SM, work rnd 1 of Chart B1 to m, SM, work rnd 53 (55, 59, 63) (67, 71) (75, 53) of Chart D (= front), SM, work rnd 1 of Chart B1 to m, RM, transfer 58 (60, 64, 68) (72, 76) (80, 84) sleeve sts onto a holder, cast on 9 (11, 11, 15) (17, 19) (21, 23) sts for underarm, SM, work rnd 1 of Chart B1 to BOR-m.

There are 212 (220, 228, 244) (256, 268) (276, 292) sts for the body.

Continue working in est pattern for back and front according to Chart D and work the new sts for underarm in sample stitch as follows:

Rnd 1: Work the next rnd of Chart D (= back) to m, SM, work the next rnd of Chart B1, p1, *k1, p1* to m (= underarm sts), SM, work the next rnd of Chart B1, SM, work the next rnd of Chart D (= front) to m, SM, work the next rnd of Chart B1, p1, *k1, p1* to m (= underarm sts), SM, work the next rnd of Chart B1 to BOR-m.

Rnd 2: Work the next rnd of Chart D (= back) to m, SM, work the next rnd of Chart B1, p to m (= underarm sts), SM, work the next rnd of Chart B1, SM, work the next rnd of Chart D (= front) to m, SM, work the next rnd of Chart B1, p to m (= underarm sts), SM, work the next rnd of Chart B1 to BOR-m.

Continue working like this (repeating rnds 1–2) until rnds 53–78 (55–78, 59–78, 63–78) (67–78, 71–78) (75–78, 53–78) of Chart D are completed.

Then continue working as established until rnds 53–78 of Chart D are completed a total of 2 (2, 2, 3) (3, 3) (3, 3) more times (or, until work measures approx. 7.5 cm / 3" less than desired total length).

Change to 3.5 mm / US 4 circular needles and work *k1 tbl, p1* ribbing until the rib hem measures 7.5 cm / 3".

Bind off using the Italian Bind-Off method (or your preferred stretchy bind-off method).

Sleeves

Transfer 58 (60, 64, 68) (72, 76) (80, 84) sleeve sts that you had on hold onto 5 mm / US 8 40–60 cm / 16–24" circular needles.

Starting from the middle of underarm, pick up and k 4 (6, 6, 8) (8, 10) (10, 12) sts, work rnd 53 (55, 59, 63) (67, 71) (75, 53) of Chart E, pick up and k 5 (5, 5, 7) (9, 9) (11, 13) sts from underarm. Place a marker to indicate the beginning of rnd (= BOR-m).

There are 67 (71, 75, 83) (89, 95) (101, 107) sts in total for the sleeve.

Rnd 1: Work the next rnd of Chart E until the last st, p1.

Continue working like this repeating rnd 1 until rnds 53–78 (55–78, 59–78, 63–78) (67–78, 71–78) (75–78, 53–78) of Chart E are completed once.

Then continue working as established until rnds 53–78 of Chart E are completed a total of 2 (2, 2, 3) (3, 3) (4, 3) more times.

Only sizes M, L, 3XL and 4XL
Work rnds 53–66 of Chart E once more.

All sizes
Change to 3.5 mm / US 4 circular needles and work one rnd as follows:
K1tog, p1, *k1 tbl, p1* to end of rnd.
1 st decreased.

There are 66 (70, 74, 82) (88, 94) (100, 106) sts in total for the sleeve.

Then work *k1 tbl, p1* ribbing until the cuff rib measures 7.5 cm / 3".

Bind off using the Italian Bind-Off method (or your preferred stretchy bind-off method).

Work the other sleeve the same.

Finishing

Fold the collar double and attach it by hand sewing loosely on the inside to prevent the neckline from becoming too tight. Weave in all loose ends.

CHART A PART 1

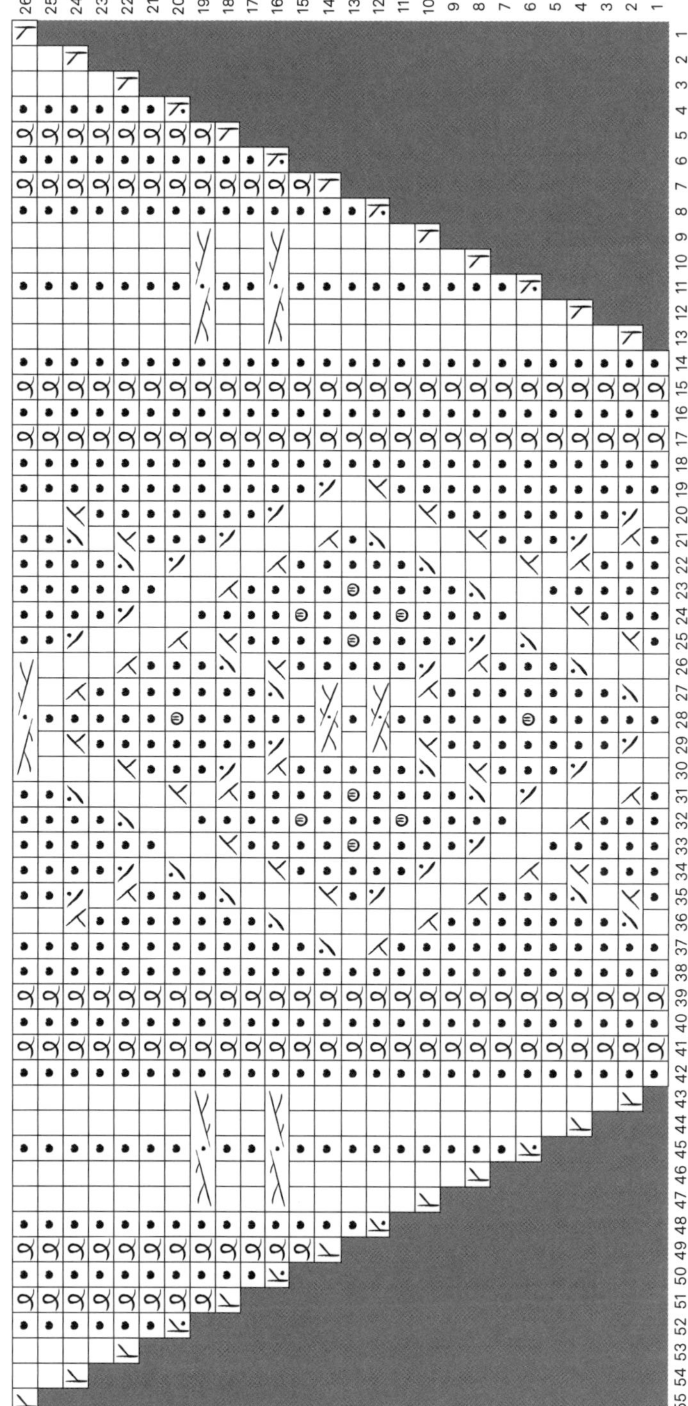

CHART A PART 2

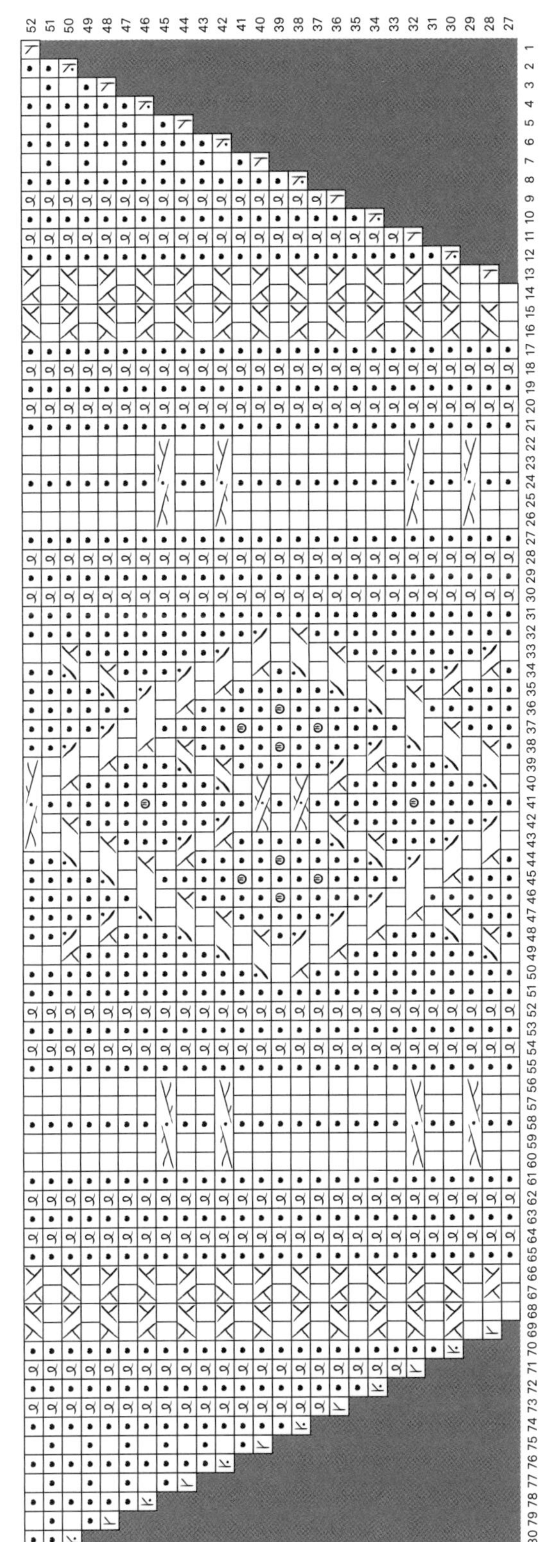

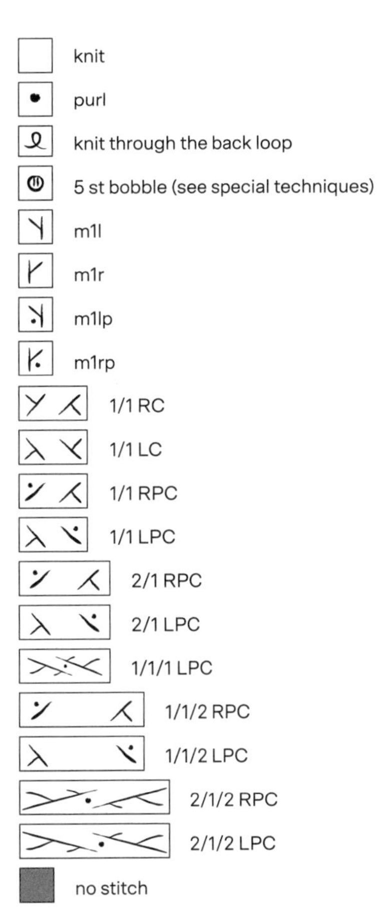

CHART B1

8	7	6	5	4	3	2	1	Row
tbl	•					•	tbl	52
tbl	•					•	tbl	51
tbl	•					•	tbl	50
tbl	•					•	tbl	49
tbl	•	2/2 LC				•	tbl	48
tbl	•					•	tbl	47
tbl	•					•	tbl	46
tbl	•					•	tbl	45
tbl	•					•	tbl	44
tbl	•					•	tbl	43
tbl	•	2/2 LC				•	tbl	42
tbl	•					•	tbl	41
tbl	•					•	tbl	40
tbl	•					•	tbl	39
tbl	•					•	tbl	38
tbl	•					•	tbl	37
tbl	•	2/2 LC				•	tbl	36
tbl	•					•	tbl	35
tbl	•					•	tbl	34
tbl	•					•	tbl	33
tbl	•					•	tbl	32
tbl	•					•	tbl	31
tbl	•	2/2 LC				•	tbl	30
tbl	•					•	tbl	29
tbl	•					•	tbl	28
tbl	•					•	tbl	27
tbl	•					•	tbl	26
tbl	•					•	tbl	25
tbl	•	2/2 LC				•	tbl	24
tbl	•					•	tbl	23
tbl	•					•	tbl	22
tbl	•					•	tbl	21
tbl	•					•	tbl	20
tbl	•					•	tbl	19
tbl	•	2/2 LC				•	tbl	18
tbl	•					•	tbl	17
tbl	•					•	tbl	16
tbl	•					•	tbl	15
tbl	•					•	tbl	14
tbl	•					•	tbl	13
tbl	•	2/2 LC				•	tbl	12
tbl	•					•	tbl	11
tbl	•					•	tbl	10
tbl	•					•	tbl	9
tbl	•					•	tbl	8
tbl	•					•	tbl	7
tbl	•	2/2 LC				•	tbl	6
tbl	•					•	tbl	5
tbl	•					•	tbl	4
tbl	•					•	tbl	3
tbl	•					•	tbl	2
tbl	•					•	tbl	1

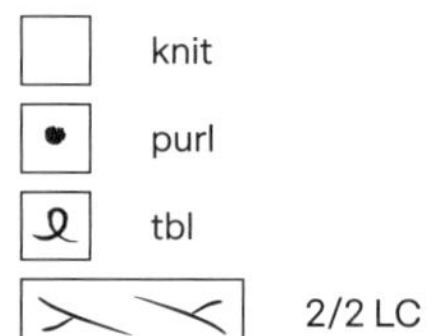

CHART B2

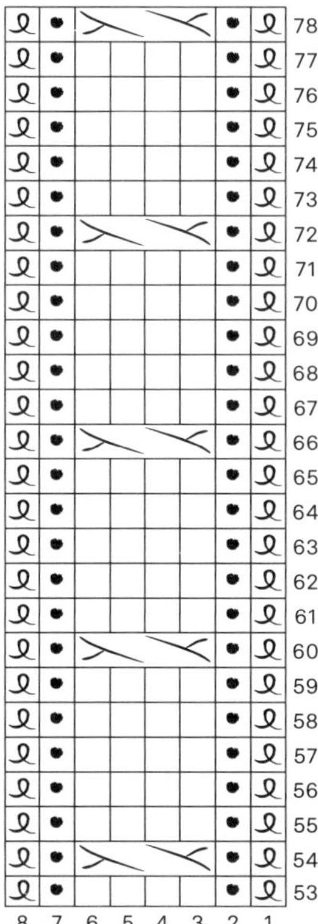

CHART C PART 1

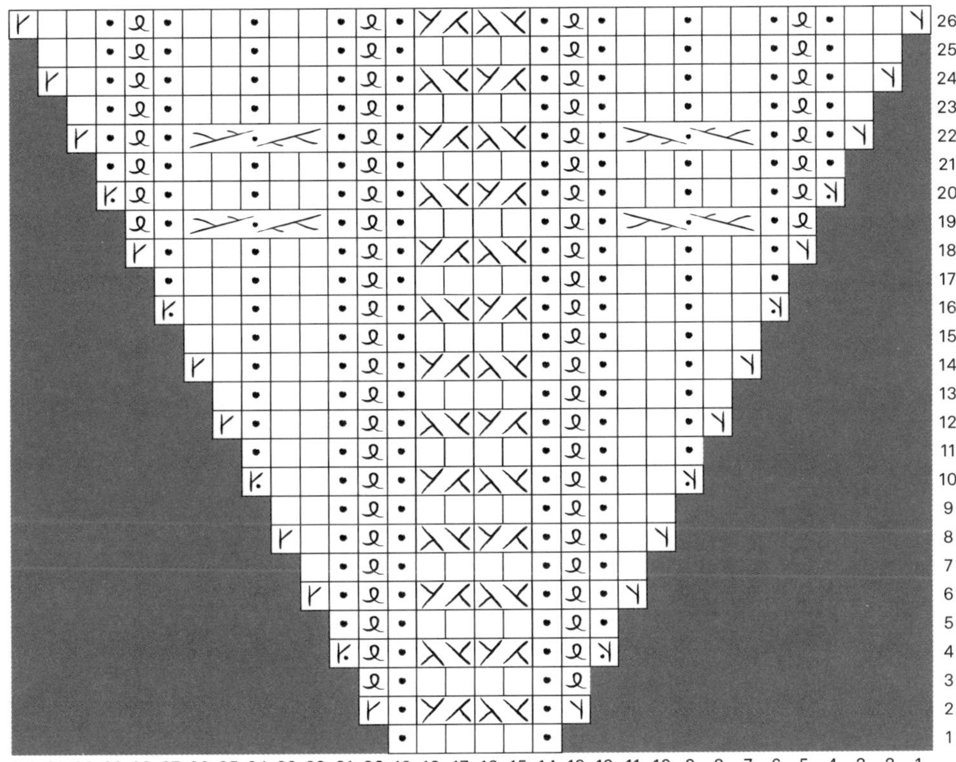

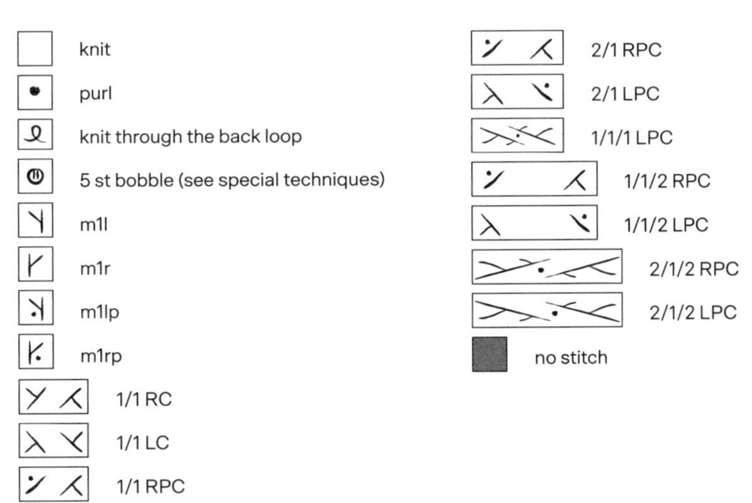

CHART C PART 2

CHART D

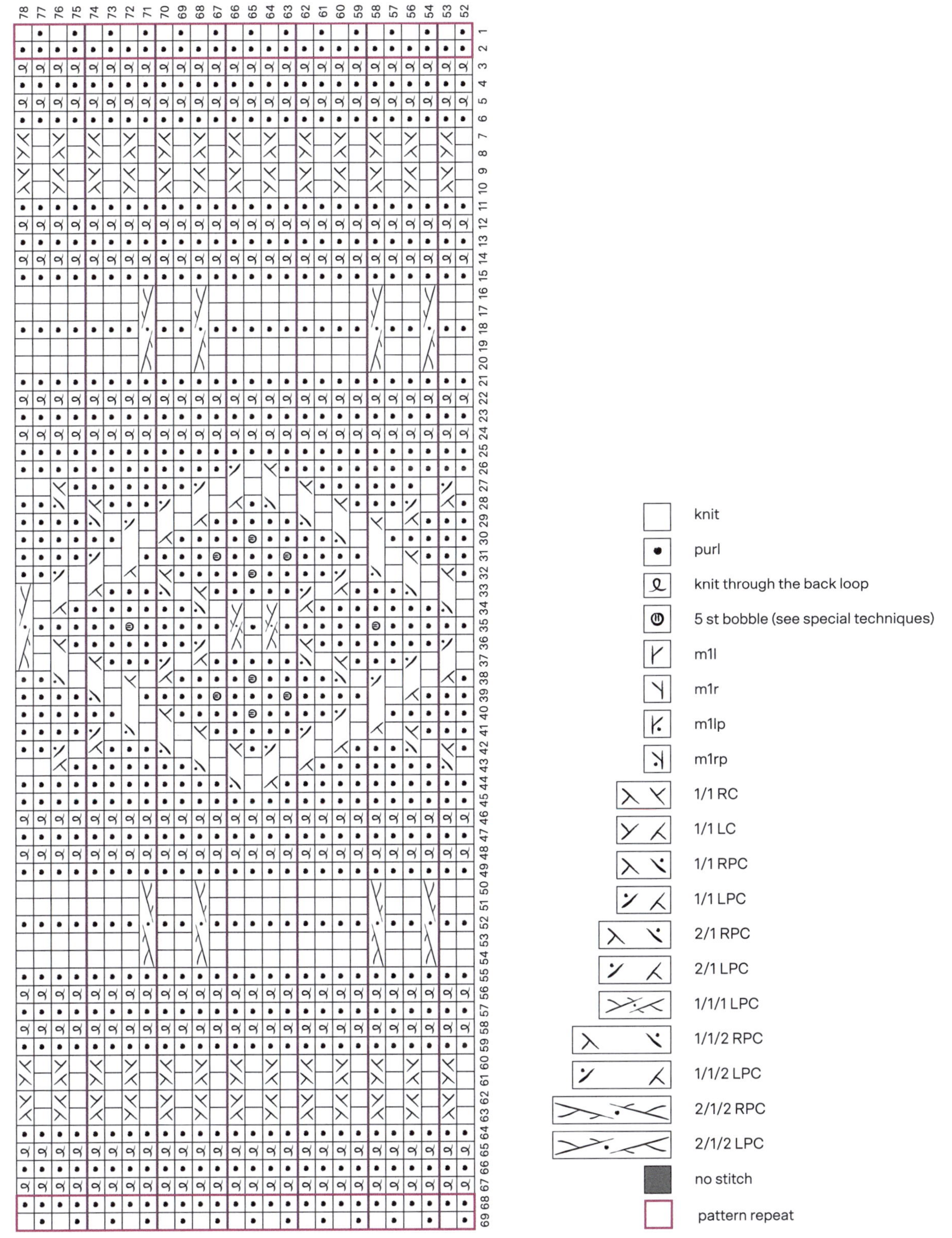

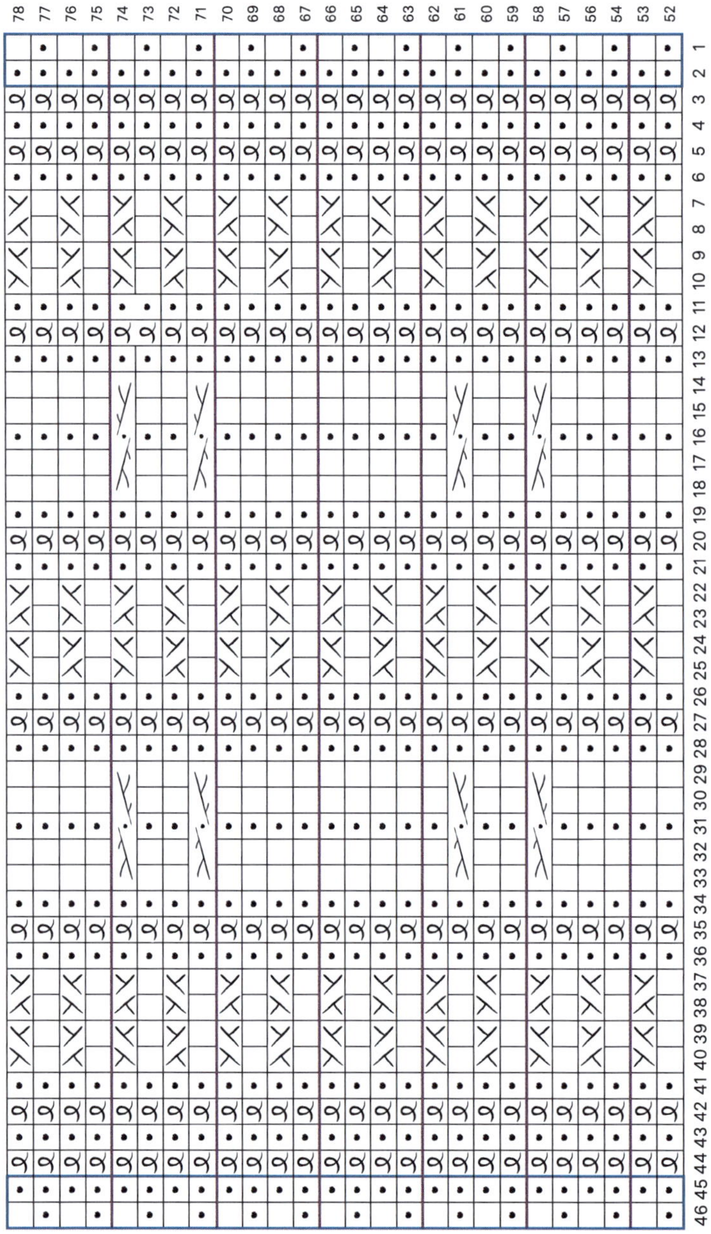

CHART E

- knit
- purl
- knit through the back loop
- 5 st bobble (see special techniques)
- m1l
- m1r
- m1lp
- m1rp
- 1/1 RC
- 1/1 LC
- 1/1 RPC
- 1/1 LPC
- 2/1 RPC
- 2/1 LPC
- 1/1/1 LPC
- 1/1/2 RPC
- 1/1/2 LPC
- 2/1/2 RPC
- 2/1/2 LPC
- no stitch
- pattern repeat

CHART F

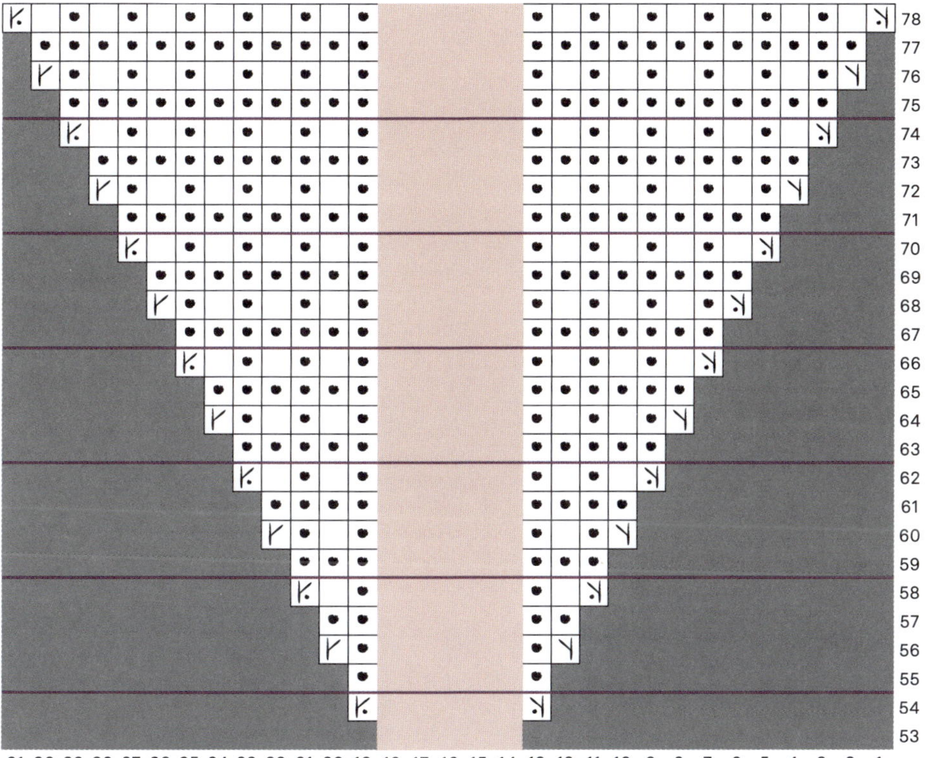

work chart D for front & back, and chart E for sleeves

Meet a sweater that's as fun to create as it is to wear! This design is a vibrant and casual addition to your knitting repertoire. The colourwork invites you to explore bold, playful patterns that dance across the fabric. With its relaxed fit and cheerful motifs, Playful Palette is perfect for those who love adding a touch of whimsy to their wardrobe. Whether you're a seasoned pro or new to colourwork, this project will tempt your needles and brighten your day with its carefree style.

PLAYFUL PALETTE

SALAD

STYLING TIP #6

Play with silhouettes by layering your knit over a shirt dress and jeans, creating unique and unexpected shapes in your outfit. This combination adds depth and intrigue, turning a simple look into a fashion-forward statement.

Sizes

XS (S, M, L) (XL, 2XL, 3XL) (4XL, 5XL)

Finished garment measurements

Bust circumference: 84 (95, 105, 116) (126, 137, 147) (158, 168.5) cm / 33 (37.5, 41.25, 45.5) (49.5, 54, 57.75) (62.25, 66.25)".

Body length from underarm to hem: 30 (31, 32, 33) (35, 38, 39) (41, 42) cm / 11.75 (12.25, 12.5, 13) (13.75, 15, 15.25) (16, 16.5)" (or desired length).

Sleeve length from underarm: 42 cm / 16.5" (or desired length).

Upper sleeve circumference: 31.5 (31.5, 31.5, 31.5) (31.5, 42, 42) (42, 42) cm / 12.5 (12.5, 12.5, 12.5) (12.5, 16.5, 16.5) (16.5, 16.5)".

Cuff circumference: 28.5 (28.5, 28.5, 28.5) (28.5, 38, 38) (38, 38) cm / 11.25 (11.25, 11.25, 11.25) (11.25, 15, 15) (15, 15)".

The sweater is designed to have 20–30 cm / 8–12" of positive ease for a relaxed fit. For a tighter fit, choose one size down.

Samples shown in size S, (Kika has a bust of approx. 89 cm / 35").

Gauge

17 sts × 26 rows / rnds = 10 cm / 4" in Stockinette st on 4.5 mm / US 7 needles, after blocking.

21 sts × 30 rnds = 10 cm / 4" in *k1 tbl, p1* rib on 3.5 mm / US 5 needles, after blocking.

Needles

3.5 mm / US 5: circular needles 40–60 cm / 16–24" for neck opening and 80–100 cm / 32–40" for hem rib, and DPNs for sleeve rib (or use the Magic Loop technique instead).

4.5 mm / US 7: circular needles 40–60 cm / 16–24" for sleeves and 80–100 cm / 32–40" for body, or just 80–100 cm / 32–40" needles if you're using the Magic Loop technique.

Notions

Removable stitch markers, tapestry needle, stitch holder or scrap yarn.

Suggested yarn

The sweater can be worked with a DK / aran / worsted weight yarn. You need approx.:

MC: 880 (1000, 1050, 1100) (1155, 1210, 1265) (1320, 1375) m / 962 (1094, 1148, 1203) (1263, 1323, 1384) (1444, 1504) yds of DK / aran / worsted weight yarn.

CC1: 70 (90, 110, 135) (165, 165, 220) (275, 275) m / 77 (98, 120, 148) (180, 180, 241) (301, 301) yds of DK / aran / worsted weight yarn.

CC2: 35 (55, 70, 85) (105, 120, 140) (155, 170) m / 38 (60, 77, 93) (115, 131, 153) (170, 186) yds of DK / aran / worsted weight yarn.

CC3: 70 (90, 110, 135) (165, 165, 220) (275, 275) m / 77 (98, 120, 148) (180, 180, 241) (301, 301) yds of DK / aran / worsted weight yarn.

Samples knitted with yarns

Light grey sample: MC: 375 (450, 475, 500) (525, 550, 575) (600, 625) g of Sandnes Garn Double Sunday (100% merino wool – 108 m / 118 yds / 50 g) in the colour 3821 **together with** 100 (110, 115, 120) (130, 135, 140) (145, 155) g of Knitting for Olive Soft Silk Mohair (70% mohair, 30% silk – 225 m / 246 yds / 25 g) in the colour Putty.

CC1: 30 (40, 50, 60) (75, 75, 100) (125, 125) g Sandnes Garn Double Sunday in the colour Peach 4033 **together with** 5 (10, 10, 15) (20, 20, 25) (30, 30) g of Knitting for Olive Soft Silk Mohair in the colour Poppy Rose.

CC2: 20 (30, 40, 50) (60, 70, 80) (90, 100) g of Säie Wool Merino Aran (100% superwash merino wool – 166 m / 181 yds / 100 g) in the colour Brilliant Mr. Fox **together with** 5 (5, 10, 10) (10, 15, 15) (20, 20) g of Säie Wool Silk Mohair (72% kid mohair, 28% silk – 840 m / 919 yds / 100 g) in the colour Brilliant Mr. Fox.

CC3: 30 (40, 50, 60) (75, 75, 100) (125, 125) g of Cascade 220 (100% wool – 200 m / 219 yds / 100 g) in the colour Olive Oil 9566 **together with** 10 (10, 15, 15) (20, 20, 25) (30, 30) g of Sandnes Garn Tynn Silk Mohair (57% mohair, 15% wool, 28% silk – 212 m / 232 yds / 25 g) in the colour Lime 9825.

The sample is worked by holding one strand of merino together with one strand of silk mohair.

Blue sample: MC: 210 (225, 250, 275) (290, 310, 325) (335, 350) g of Filcolana Arwetta (80% wool, 20% nylon – 210 m / 230 yds / 50 g) in the colour 340 **together with** 75 (80, 90, 95) (100, 110, 115) (115, 125) g of Krea Deluxe Silk Mohair (45% silk, 33% mohair, 22% alpaca – 240 m / 262 yds/ 20 g) in the colour 24 **together with** 105 (110, 125, 135) (145, 155, 160) (165, 175) g of Isager Silk Mohair (75% kid mohair, 25% silk – 212 m / 232 yds / 25 g) in the colour 41.

CC1: 10 (15, 20, 30) (30, 40, 45) (55, 55) g of Filcolana Arwetta in the colour 101 **together with** 10 (10, 15, 15) (20, 20, 25) (30, 35) g of Filcolana Tilia (70% kid mohair, 30% silk – 210 m / 230 yds / 25 g) in the colour 101.

CC2: 15 (30, 40, 50) (60, 70, 80) (90, 100) g of Knitting for Olive Merino (100% merino wool – 250 m / 273 yds / 50 g) in the colour Mustard **together with** 5 (10, 15, 20) (20, 25, 25) (30, 30) g Filcolana Tilia in the colour 136.

CC3: 20 (25, 30, 35) (40, 45, 55) (60, 70) g of Knitting for Olive Merino in the colour Lead **together with** 10 (10, 15, 15) (20, 20, 25) (30, 35) g of Knitting for Olive Soft Silk Mohair (70% mohair, 30% silk – 225 m / 246 yds / 25 g) in the colour Lead.

The sample is worked by holding one strand of merino together with two strands of silk mohair.

DIRECTIONS

The sweater is worked top down seamlessly. The collar is worked in a twisted rib stitch to double length and folded in half at the end, this gives the sweater more structure and a put together feel. The sleeves are wide and worked without decreases for a relaxed and contemporary vibe.

Collar

Cast on 96 (104, 108, 108) (108, 112, 112) (116, 116) sts loosely with MC using the Backwards Loop Cast-On method with 3.5 mm / US 5 (40–60 cm / 16–24) circular needles (the collar will be folded double and attached on the inside by hand sewing at the end). Place a marker to indicate the beginning of rnd (=BOR-m).

Work *k1 tbl, p1* rib in the rnd until the collar measures 9 cm / 3.5" in total.

Yoke

Change to 4.5 mm / US 7 circular needles and work one set-up rnd in MC as follows:

Set-up rnd:
Sizes XS and S: K to end of rnd.

Size M: *K27, M1L* to end of rnd. 4 sts increased.
Size L: *K9, M1L * to end of rnd. 12 sts increased.
Size XL: K2, M1L, k2, M1L, k2, M1L, *k6, M1L* to end of rnd. 20 sts increased.
Size 2XL: K1, M1L, k1, M1L, *k5, M1L* to end of rnd. 24 sts increased.
Size 3XL: K1, M1L, k1, M1L, k2, M1L, *k4, M1L* to last 4 sts, k1, M1L, k1, M1L, k2, M1L. 32 sts increased.
Size 4XL: K4, *k3, M1L* to last 4 sts, k4. 36 sts increased.
Size 5XL: K1, M1L, k1, M1L, k1, M1L, k2, M1L, k2, M1L, *k3, M1L* to last 7 sts, k1, M1L, k1, M1L, k1, M1L, k2, M1L, k2, M1L. 44 sts increased.

There are 96 (104, 112, 120) (128, 136, 144) (152, 160) sts in total.

Start working according to Chart A across all sts (**Note!** Chart A has increases in the chart), sts 1–10 in the chart repeats a total of 24 (26, 28, 30) (32, 34, 36) (38, 40) times around the yoke.

Work until all rnds 1–50 of Chart A are completed.

There are 240 (260, 280, 300) (320, 340, 360) (380, 400) sts in total.

Continue working in Stockinette st in MC for 4 (8, 10, 14) (14, 18, 20) (24, 26) more rnds [or until Stockinette st part in MC measures approx. 1.5 (3, 4, 5) (5, 7, 8) (9, 10) cm / 0.5 (1.25, 1.5, 2) (2, 2.75, 3.25) (3.75, 4)" from the end of Chart A pattern motif].

Body

Next, we're going to knit the body and put the sts for the sleeves on hold.

Continue in MC as follows:
K70 (80, 90, 100) (110, 110, 120) (130, 140) (= back sts), transfer 50 (50, 50, 50) (50, 60, 60) (60, 60) sleeve sts onto a stitch holder or a piece of scrap yarn, cast on 10 (10, 10, 10) (10, 20, 20) (20, 20) sts for underarm with the Backwards Loop Cast-On method, k70 (80, 90, 100) (110, 110, 120) (130, 140) (= front sts), transfer 50 (50, 50, 50) (50, 60, 60) (60, 60) sleeve sts onto a stitch holder or a piece of scrap yarn, cast on 10 (10, 10, 10) (10, 20, 20) (20, 20) sts for underarm, place new BOR-m.

There are 160 (180, 200, 220) (240, 260, 280) (300, 320) sts in total for body.

Then work in Stockinette st in MC until the body measures 22 (23, 24, 25) (27, 30, 31) (32, 34) cm / 8.5 (9, 9.5, 10) (10.5, 12, 12) (12.5, 13)" from the underarm (or until 8 cm / 3" less than desired total length).

Work one rnd of decreases as follows:

Decrease rnd: *K8, k2tog*, repeat *–* to end.

There are 144 (162, 180, 198) (216, 234, 252) (270, 288) sts in total.

Change to 3.5 mm / US 5 circular needles and work *k1 tbl, p1* rib until the hem measures 8 cm.

Bind off using the Standard Bind-Off method, (or your preferred bind-off method).

Sleeves

Transfer the 50 (50, 50, 50) (50, 60, 60) (60, 60) sleeve sts that you had on hold onto 4.5 mm / US 7 (40–60 cm / 16–24") circular needles, double-pointed needles, or longer circular needles for the Magic Loop technique.

With MC and starting from the middle of underarm, pick up and k5 (5, 5, 5) (5, 10, 10) (10, 10) sts, k50 (50, 50, 50) (50, 60, 60) (60, 60) sleeve sts, pick up and k5 (5, 5, 5) (5, 10, 10) (10, 10) sts. Place a marker to indicate the beginning of rnd (= BOR-m).

There are 60 (60, 60, 60) (60, 80, 80) (80, 80) sts in total for the sleeve.

With MC, work the sleeve in Stockinette st until the sleeve measured from the underarm is 36 cm / 14" (or 8 cm / 3" less than total desired length).

Change to 3.5 mm / US 5 (40 cm / 16") circular needles, double-pointed needles, or longer circular needles for the Magic Loop technique.

Work *k1 tbl, p1* rib until the cuff measures 8 cm / 3".

Bind off using the Standard Bind-Off method, (or your preferred bind-off method).

Work the other sleeve the same way.

Finishing

Fold the collar double and attach the collar on the inside by hand sewing it together loosely, being careful not to tighten it too much – you'll want to fit it over your head easily. Weave in all ends.

CHART A

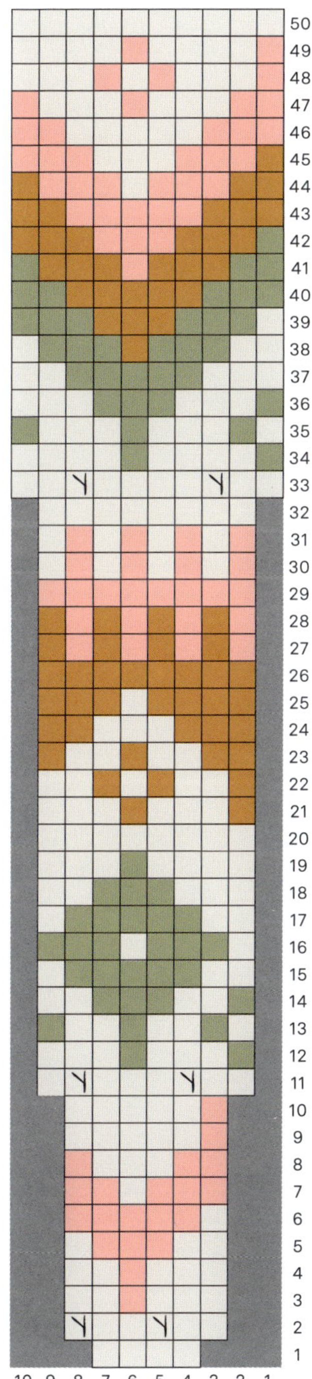

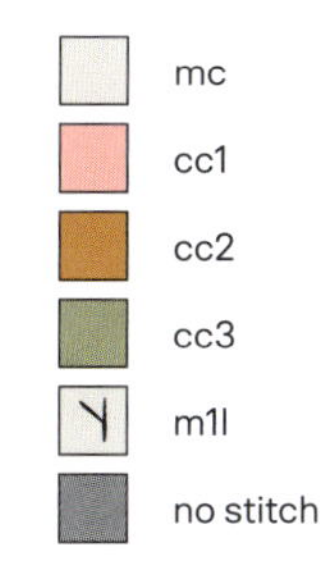

This sweater is the perfect modern knit with a romantic twist. Its boxy shape gives it a laid-back fit and a contemporary feel. The subtle all-over lace pattern and delicate cable details on the sleeve cuffs and hem add an elegant finishing touch. With a cropped fit and slim sleeves, this flattering sweater is easy to style for both casual and dressed-up occasions.

TAKE ME OUT

15

Sizes

XXS (XS, S, M) (L, XL, 2XL) (3XL, 4XL, 5XL)

Finished garment measurements

Bust circumference: 101 (113, 124.5, 136.5) (148, 160, 172) (183.5, 195.5, 207) cm / 39.75 (44.5, 49, 53.75) (58.25, 63, 67.5) (72.25, 77, 81.5)".

Body length from underarm to hem: 38 (38, 38, 38) (42, 42, 42) (48, 48, 48) cm / 15 (15, 15, 15) (16.5, 16.5, 16.5) (19, 19, 19)".

Sleeve length underarm to cuff: 47.5 cm / 18.75" all sizes (or desired length).

Upper sleeve circumference: 35.5 (35.5, 35.5, 41) (41, 41, 47) (47, 47, 47) cm / 14 (14, 14, 16.25) (16.25, 16.25, 18.5) (18.5, 18.5, 18.5)".

Sleeve cuff circumference: 25 (25, 25, 29) (29, 29, 33.5) (33.5, 33.5, 33.5) cm / 9.75 (9.75, 9.75, 11.5) (11.5, 11.5, 13.25) (13.25, 13.25, 13.25)".

The Take Me Out sweater is designed to have 20–30 cm / 7.75–11.75" of positive ease.

The light green sample shown in size S (Kika has a bust of approx. 89 cm / 35"), the peach sample shown in size L (Juki has a bust of approx. 115 cm / 45").

Gauge

17 sts × 24 rows/rnds = 10 cm / 4" on 5 mm / US 8 needles in Stockinette st, after blocking.

24 sts × 30 rnds = 10 cm / 4" on 3.5 mm / US 4 needles in Chart C cable stitch pattern, after blocking.

Needles

3.5 mm / US 4: circular needles 40–60 cm / 16–24" for cuffs and collar, and 80–100 cm / 32–40" for hem, or just 80–100 cm / 32–40" needles if you're using the Magic Loop technique.

5 mm / US 8: circular needles 40–60 cm / 16–24" for sleeves and 80–100 cm / 32–40" for body, or just 80–100 cm / 32–40" needles if you're using the Magic Loop technique.

Notions

Removable stitch markers, stitch wire or scrap yarn, tapestry needle, DPN or cable needle for hem and cuffs.

Suggested yarn

The sweater can be worked with one strand of DK or sport weight yarn, or by holding two strands of fingering weight yarn together (light green sample), or by holding one strand of fingering yarn with two strands of lace weight yarn together (peach sample).

You need approx. 875 (1000, 1250, 1500) (1625, 1750, 1875) (2000, 2125, 2250) m / 957 (1094, 1367, 1640) (1776, 1912, 2048) (2187, 2323, 2459) yds of DK or Sport weight yarn or 1750 (2000, 2500, 3000) (3250, 3500, 3750) (4000, 4250, 4500) m / 1912 (2187, 2734, 3281) (3556, 3832, 4107) (4374, 4650, 4925) yds of fingering weight yarn or 3500 (4000, 5000, 6000) (6500, 7000, 7500) (8000, 8500, 9000) m / 3832 (4374, 5468, 6562) (7108, 7655, 8202) (8749, 9296, 9842) yds of lace weight yarn.

Samples knitted with yarns

Light green: 175 (200, 250, 300) (325, 350, 375) (400, 425, 450) g of Drops Brushed Alpaca Silk (77% alpaca, 23% silk – 140 m / 153 yds / 25 g) in the colour 27 held **together**

with 155 (180, 225, 270) (290, 315, 335) (355, 380, 400) g of Knitting for Olive Merino (100% merino wool – 250 m / 273 yds / 50 g) in the colour Fennel Seed.

The sample is worked by holding one strand of merino together with one strand of brushed alpaca.

Peach sample: 155 (180, 225, 270) (290, 315, 335) (355, 380, 400) g of Knitting for Olive Merino (100% merino wool – 250 m / 273 yds / 50 g) in the colour Soft Peach **together with** 200 (225, 280, 340) (365, 390, 420) (450, 475, 500) g of Knitting for Olive Silk Mohair (70% mohair, 30% silk – 225 m / 246 yds / 25 g) in the colour Soft Peach.

The sample is worked by holding two strands of silk mohair together with one strand of merino.

DIRECTIONS

The sweater is worked top down seamlessly. First, the upper back is worked flat and then stitches are picked up for each front separately. The body is worked in the round and the stitches for the sleeves are picked up and worked in the round. Lastly, the stitches for the collar are picked up. The collar is folded double and sewn at the end.

Upper Back

Cast on 80 (90, 100, 110) (120, 130, 140) (150, 160, 170) sts with the Backwards Loop Cast-On method with 5 mm / US 8 (80–100 cm / 32–40") circular needles. Do not join to work in the rnd.

Work one Set-up row and place 2 removable stitch markers to mark where sts will be picked up for the Left and Right Front later. Work as follows:

Set-up row (WS): P30 (32, 37, 42) (47, 52, 55) (60, 65, 70), PM around the strand between the sts, p20 (26, 26, 26) (26, 26, 30) (30, 30 30) (= neckline sts), PM around the strand between the sts, p30 (32, 37, 42) (47, 52, 55) (60, 65, 70).

Starting with a k row, work 6 rows of Stockinette st (your last row is a WS row).

Next, start working according to Chart A1 or A2 depending on your chosen size as follows:

Sizes XXS (XS, S)
Rows 1–42: Work Chart A1 (A2, A1) rows 1–28 once, then work rows 1–14 once [the chart repeats across all sts 4 (4, 4) times].

Sizes M (L, XL, 2XL)
Rows 1–56: Work Chart A2 (A1, A2, A1) rows 1–28, twice [the charts repeats across all sts 5 (6, 6, 7) times].

Sizes (3XL, 4XL, 5XL)
Rows 1–70: Work Chart (A2, A1, A2) rows 1–28 twice, then work rows 1–14 once [the charts repeats across all sts (7, 8, 8) times].

The Upper Back is complete. Cut the yarn and leave the sts on hold while working the Upper Front next.

Left Upper Front

Next, sts are picked up for the Left Upper Front along the left shoulder from the Upper Back. The Left Upper Front is worked flat according to Chart A (choose Chart A1 or A2 depending on your chosen size) while the neckline is shaped by working increases.

With the RS facing, pick up and k30 (32, 37, 42) (47, 52, 55) (60, 65, 70) sts from the left side stitch marker (= neckline marker) placed at the cast-on edge at the beginning of the Upper Back to the left outer edge with

5 mm / US 8 needles. You can remove this marker now.

Starting with a p row, work 9 rows of Stockinette st (last row is a WS row).

Start shaping the neckline by working increases as follows:

Row 1 (RS): K2, M1L, k8 (0, 15, 10) (5, 0, 13) (8, 3, 18), work row 1 of Chart A1 (A2, A1, A2) (A1, A2, A1) (A2, A1, A2) to end.
1 st increased.
Row 2 (WS): P all sts.
Row 3: K2, M1L, k9 (1, 16, 11) (6, 1, 14) (9, 4, 19), work row 3 of Chart A1 (A2, A1, A2) (A1, A2, A1) (A2, A1, A2) to end.
1 st increased.
Row 4: P all sts.
Row 5: K2, M1L, k10 (2, 17, 12) (7, 2, 15) (10, 5, 20), work row 5 of Chart A1 (A2, A1, A2) (A1, A2, A1) (A2, A1, A2) to end.
1 st increased.
Row 6: P all sts.
Row 7: K2, M1L, k to end. 1 st increased.
Row 8: P all sts.
Row 9: K2, M1L, k to end. 1 st increased.
Row 10: P all sts.
Row 11: K2, M1L, k to end. 1 st increased.
Row 12: P all sts.

There are 36 (38, 43, 48) (53, 58, 61) (66, 71, 76) sts in total.

The Left Upper Front is complete. Cut the yarn and leave the sts on hold while working the Right Upper Front next.

Right Upper Front

Next, sts are picked up for the Right Upper Front along the right shoulder from the Upper Back. The Right Upper Front is worked flat according to Chart A (choose Chart A1 or A2 depending on your chosen size) while the neckline is shaped by working increases.

With the RS facing, pick up and k30 (32, 37, 42) (47, 52, 55) (60, 65, 70) sts from the right outer edge to the right side stitch marker (= neckline marker) placed at the cast-on edge at the beginning of the Upper Back with 5 mm / US 8 needles. You can remove this marker now.

Starting with a p row, work 9 rows of Stockinette st (the last row is a WS row).

Start shaping the neckline by working increases as follows:

Row 1 (RS): Work row 1 of Chart A1 (A2, A1, A2) (A1, A2, A1) (A2, A1, A2) to last 10 (2, 17, 12) (7, 2, 15) (10, 5, 20) sts, k to last 2 sts, M1R, k2. 1 st increased.
Row 2 (WS): P all sts.
Row 3: Work row 3 of Chart A1 (A2, A1, A2) (A1, A2, A1) (A2, A1, A2) to last 11 (3, 18, 13) (8, 3, 16) (11, 6, 21) sts, k to last 2 sts, M1R, k2.
1 st increased.
Row 4: P all sts.
Row 5: Work row 5 of Chart A1 (A2, A1, A2) (A1, A2, A1) (A2, A1, A2) to last 12 (4, 19, 14) (9, 4, 17) (12, 7, 22) sts, k to last 2 sts, M1R, k2.1 st increased.
Row 6: P all sts.
Row 7: K until last 2 sts, M1R, k2. 1 st increased.
Row 8: P all sts.
Row 9: K until last 2 sts, M1R, k2. 1 st increased.
Row 10: P all sts.
Row 11: K until last 2 sts, M1R, k2. 1 st increased.
Row 12: P all sts.

There are 36 (38, 43, 48) (53, 58, 61) (66, 71, 76) sts in total.

The Right Upper Front is complete. Don't cut the yarn yet.

Joining the Right and Left Upper Front

Next, the Right and Left Upper Front sts are joined together to work the Upper Front body flat, new sts are cast on for the middle of the neckline. Transfer the Left Upper Front sts that you had on hold onto the working needles and work as follows across the Left and Right Upper front sts:

Joining row (RS): K across all the Right Upper Front sts, cast on 8 (14, 14, 14) (14, 14, 18) (18, 18, 18) sts for the middle of the neckline with the Backwards Loop Cast-On method, join the Left Upper Front sts and k to end.

There are 80 (90, 100, 110) (120, 130, 140) (150, 160, 170) sts in total.

Set-up row (WS): P all sts.

Continue working the Upper front according to Chart A1 (A2, A1, A2) (A1, A2, A1) (A2, A1, A2) in your chosen size as follows:

Sizes XXS (XS, S)
Rows 15–42: Work Chart A1 (A2, A1) rows 15–28, then work rows 1–14.

Sizes M (L, XL, 2XL)
Rows 15–56: Work Chart A2 (A1, A2, A1) rows 15–28, then work rows 1–28.

Sizes 3XL (4XL, 5XL)
Rows 15–70: Work Chart A2 (A1, A2) rows 15–28, then work rows 1–28, and then work rows 1–14.

The Upper Front is complete. Don't cut the yarn yet.

Body

Next, the Upper Front and Upper Back sts are joined together to work the lower body in the rnd.

Joining rnd: Upper Front sts: work rnd 15 (15, 15, 1) (1, 1, 1) (15, 15, 15) of Chart A1 (A2, A1, A2) (A1, A2, A1) (A2, A1, A2) [the chart repeats 4 (4, 4, 5) (6, 6, 7) (7, 8, 8) times across all sts], PM, cast on 6 sts for the underarm with the Backwards Loop Cast-On method, PM, Upper Back sts: work rnd 15 (15, 15, 1) (1, 1, 1) (15, 15, 15) of Chart A1 (A2, A1, A2) (A1, A2, A1) (A2, A1, A2) [the chart repeats 4 (4, 4, 5) (6, 6, 7) (7, 8, 8) times across all sts], PM, cast on 6 sts for the underarm, PM (= BOR-m).

There are 172 (192, 212, 232) (252, 272, 292) (312, 332, 352) body sts in total.

Rnd 1: Work rnd 16 (16, 16, 2) (2, 2, 2) (16, 16, 16) of Chart A1 (A2, A1, A2) (A1, A2, A1) (A2, A1, A2) to m, SM, p1, k4, p1, SM, work rnd 16 (16, 16, 2) (2, 2, 2) (16, 16, 16) of Chart A1 (A2, A1, A2) (A1, A2, A1) (A2, A1, A2) to m, SM, p1, k4, p1.

Rnd 2: Work the next rnd of Chart A1 (A2, A1, A2) (A1, A2, A1) (A2, A1, A2) to m, SM, work rnd 1 of Chart B, SM, work the next rnd of Chart A1 (A2, A1, A2) (A1, A2, A1) (A2, A1, A2) to m, SM, work Rnd 1 of Chart B.

Rnd 3: Work the next rnd of Chart A1 (A2, A1, A2) (A1, A2, A1) (A2, A1, A2) to m, SM, work the next rnd of Chart B, SM, work the next rnd of Chart A1 (A2, A1, A2) (A1, A2, A1) (A2, A1, A2) to m, SM, work the next rnd of Chart B.

Repeat rnd 3 two more times (meaning you'll have completed Chart B rows 1-4 once).

Sizes XXS (XS, S) (3XL, 4XL, 5X) Continue in this manner: repeat rnds 2–5 above while repeating rnds 1–4 of Chart B (= underarm sts) and always working the next rnd of Chart A1 (A2, A1) (A2, A1, A2) until rnds 16–28 are complete.

Sizes M (L, XL, XL)
Continue in this manner: repeat rnds 2–5 above while repeating rnds 1–4 of Chart B (= underarm sts) and always working the next rnd of Chart A2 (A1, A2, A1) until rnds 2–28 are complete.

All sizes
Continue as established and work rnds 1–28 of Chart A1 (A2, A1, A2) (A1, A2, A1) (A2, A1, A2) a total of 2 (2, 2, 2) (2, 2, 2) (3, 3, 3) more times and working rnds 1–4 of Chart B as many times as necessary, or until body measured from underarm is approx. 8 cm / 3.25" less than total desired length.

Change to 3.5 mm / US 4 (80–100 cm / 32–40") circular needles for the hem and work as follows:

Rnd 1: *K4, p1* to 5 sts before m, k4, p2tog (you need to remove the marker between the sts to do the p2tog), work rnd 1 of Chart C to m (= underarm sts), RM, *k4, p1* to last 5 sts before m, k4, p2tog (you need to remove the marker between the sts to do the p2tog), work rnd 1 of Chart C (= underarm sts) to end of rnd.

2 sts decreased, there are 170 (190, 210, 230) (250, 270, 290) (310, 330, 350) body sts in total.

Rnd 2: Work rnd 2 of Chart C to end of rnd.
Rnd 3: Work rnd 3 of Chart C to end of rnd.
Rnd 4: Work rnd 4 of Chart C to end of rnd.
Rnd 5: Work rnd 1 of Chart C to end of rnd.

Repeat rnds 2–5 five more times. Then work rnds 2–3 once more.

Bind off all sts using the Standard Bind-Off method (or your preferred bind-off method).

Sleeves

For the sleeves, sts are picked up and worked along the armhole openings. The sleeves are worked in the rnd on either 5 mm / US 8 (40–60 cm / 16–24") circular needles, double-pointed needles or longer circular needles for the Magic Loop technique. With the RS facing, starting from the middle of the underarm, pick up and k 60 (60, 60, 70) (70, 70, 80) (80, 80, 80) sts evenly along the armhole opening. Place a marker to mark the beginning of rnd (= BOR-m).

Work 6 rnds of Stockinette st. Continue and work the sleeve according to Chart A1 (A1, A1, A2) (A2, A2, A1) (A1, A1, A1) in the rnd until the sleeve measures 38.5 cm / 15" from underarm (or until the sleeve measures approx. 8 cm / 3" less than total desired length).

Change to 3.5 mm / US4 DPNs or circular needles (for Magic Loop technique) for the cuffs and work as follows:

Rnd 1: Work rnd 3 of Chart C to end of rnd.
Rnd 2: Work rnd 4 of Chart C to end of rnd.
Rnd 3: Work rnd 1 of Chart C to end of rnd.
Rnd 4: Work rnd 2 of Chart C to end of rnd.

Repeat rnds 1–4 five more times. Then work rnds 1–2 once more.

Bind off all sts using the Standard Bind-Off method (or your preferred bind-off method).

Work the other sleeve the same way.

Collar

For the collar, sts are picked up along the neckline and a 1 × 1 rib is worked with 3.5 mm / US 4 (40–60 cm / 16–24") circular needles.

Begin picking up sts at one of the seams between the Upper Front and Upper Back. Pick up and k 72 (84, 84, 84) (84, 84, 92) (92, 92, 92) sts evenly around the neckline (the rhythm for picking up sts is 1 st for every st / row). Place a marker to indicate the beginning of rnd.

Work *k1, p1* ribbing until the collar measures 9 cm / 3.5".

Bind off loosely using the Standard Bind-Off method.

Finishing

Fold the collar double and attach it on the inside by sewing it loosely to the pick-up edge. Weave in all ends.

STYLING TIP #7
Tuck your knit into your pants or skirt to create a defined waist and enhance your silhouette. This simple trick adds structure, balancing the volume of your knit with a flattering shape.

CHART A1

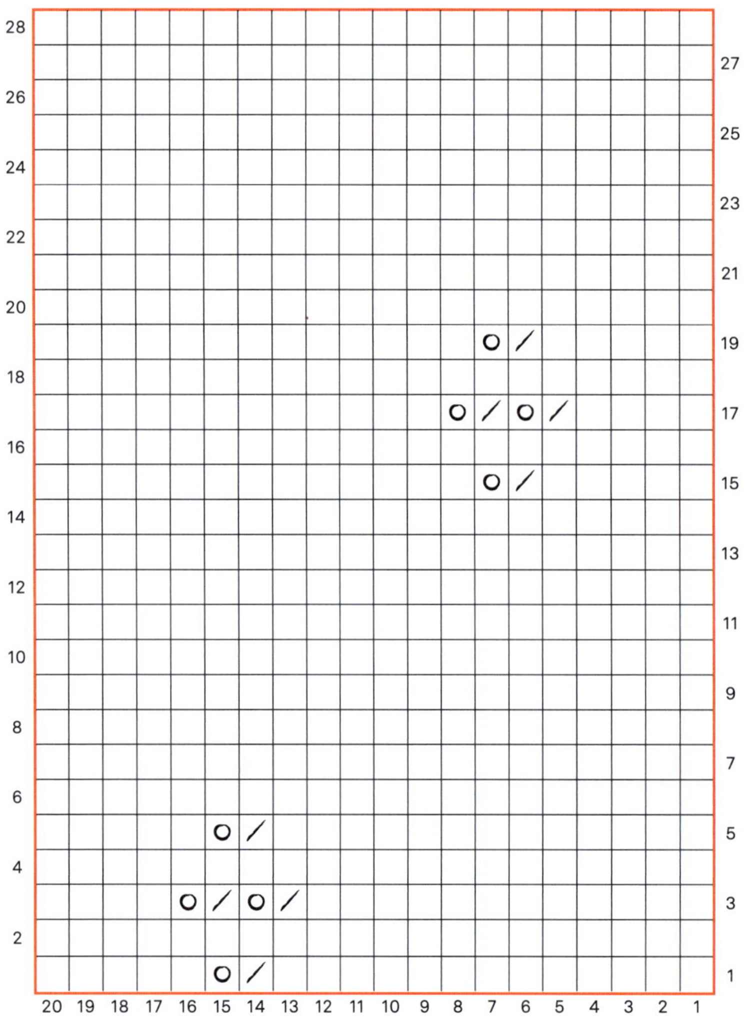

- ☐ rs: knit, ws: purl
- ⁄ knit 2 together
- O yo
- ☐ pattern repeat

CHART A2

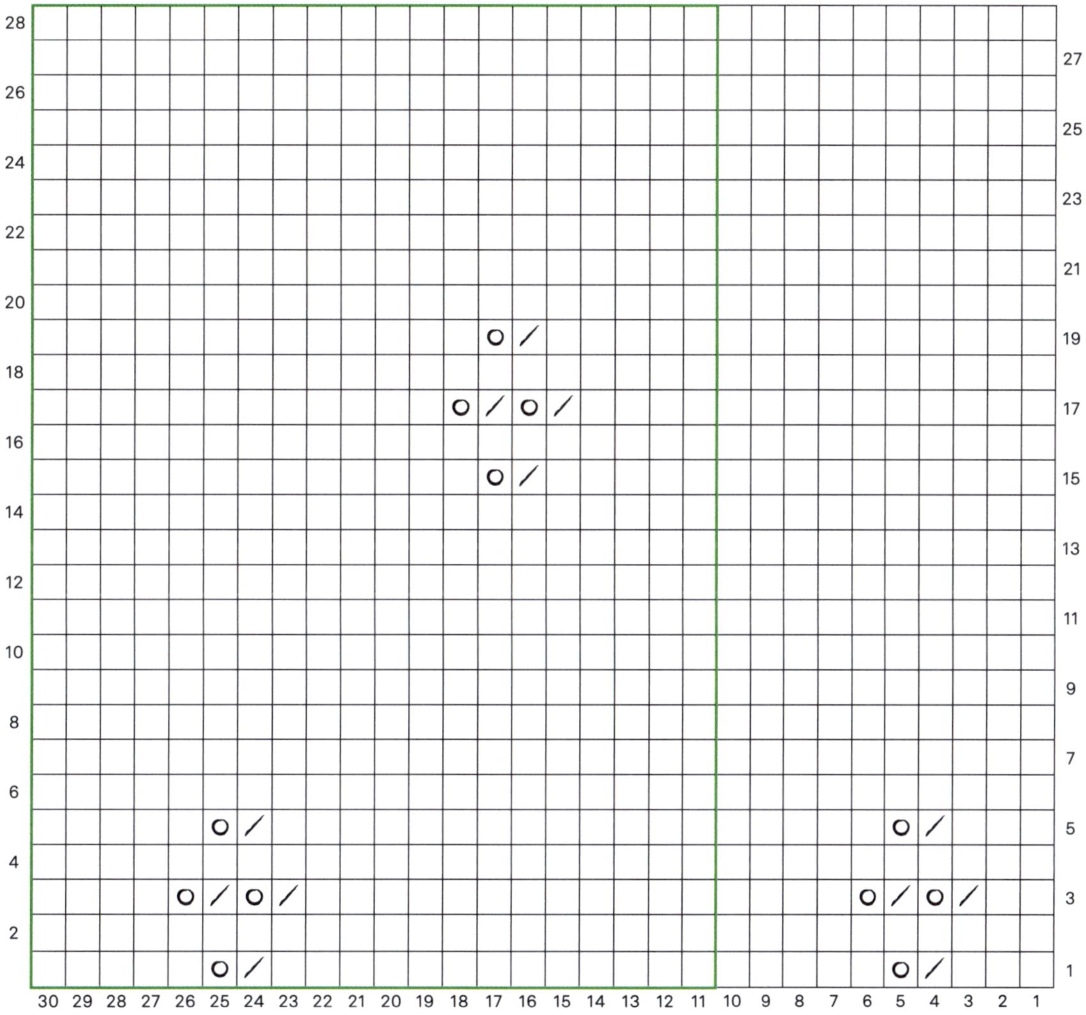

	30	29	28	27	26	25	24	23	22	21	20	19	18	17	16	15	14	13	12	11	10	9	8	7	6	5	4	3	2	1	
28																															
																															27
26																															
																															25
24																															
																															23
22																															
																															21
20																															
													O	/																	19
18																															
												O	/	O	/																17
16																															
													O	/																	15
14																															
																															13
12																															
																															11
10																															
																															9
8																															
																															7
6																															
						O	/																			O	/				5
4																															
					O	/	O	/																	O	/	O	/			3
2																															
						O	/																			O	/				1

CHART B

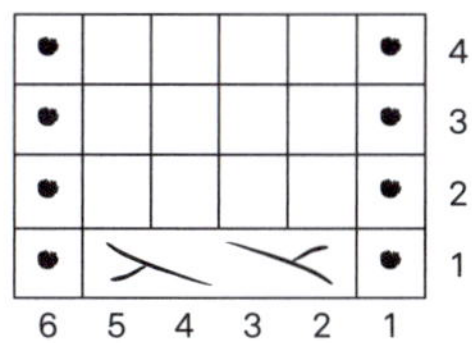

CHART C

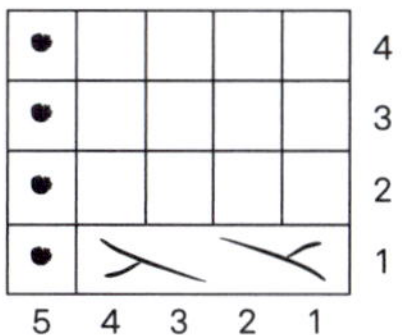

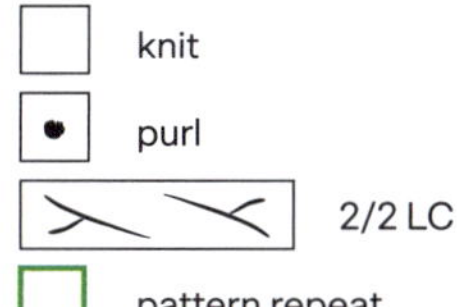

A decorative lace and cable motif adorns the back, front and sleeves of this cardigan. With dropped shoulders and seamless construction from the top down, the length of the Limoncello cardigan is easy to customise. The optional pockets add a playful finishing touch and are a fun detail.

LIMON-
CELLO

Sizes

XS (S, M, L) (XL, 2XL, 3XL) (4XL, 5XL)

Finished garment measurements

Bust circumference (including front edge plackets when worn open): 113.5 (121, 130, 137.5) (143.5, 148.5, 153.5) (158.5, 165) cm / 44.75 (47.75, 51.25, 54.25) (56.5, 58.5, 60.5) (62.5, 65)".

Length from underarm to hem: 21.5 (26, 28, 31.5) (31.5, 33.5, 36) (36, 38.5) cm / 8.5 (10.25, 11, 12.5) (12.5, 13.25, 14) (14, 15)".

Sleeve length from underarm to hem: 54 cm / 12.25".

Upper sleeve circumference: 34 (34, 40, 40) (40, 40, 40) (46, 46) cm / 13.5 (13.5, 15.75, 15.75) (15.75, 15.75, 15.75) (18, 18)".

Cuff circumference: 21 (21, 26, 26) (26, 26, 26) (31, 31) cm / 8.25 (8.25, 10.25, 10.25) (10.25, 10.25, 10.25) (12.25, 12.25)".

The Limoncello cardigan is designed to have about 20–30 cm / 8–12" of positive ease for a relaxed fit.

Yellow sample shown in size M (Kika has a bust of approx. 89 cm / 35").

Gauge

16 sts × 24 rows/rnds = 10 cm / 4" in Stockinette st flat on 5 mm / US 8 needles, after blocking.

20 sts × 34 rows/rnds = 10 cm / 4" in 1 × 1 rib flat on 3 mm / US 2.5 needles, after blocking.

Needles

3 mm / US2.5: circular needles 80–100 cm / 32–40" for rib hem, and DPNs for sleeve rib cuffs and button band (or use the Magic Loop technique).

5 mm / US8: circular needles 80–100 cm / 32–40" for body, and circular needles 40 cm / 16" for sleeves or DPNs (or use the Magic Loop technique).

Notions

Removable stitch markers, tapestry needle, stitch holder or scrap yarn, 5 buttons (2.5 cm / 1" diameter), optional: cable needle (or use a DPN).

Suggested yarn

The cardigan is knitted with one strand of sport or DK weight yarn together with a lace weight yarn.

You need approx. 1050 (1125, 1200, 1275) (1350, 1425, 1500) (1575, 1650) m / 1149 (1230, 1312, 1393) (1476, 1557, 1640) (1721, 1803) yds of sport or DK weight yarn **together with** 1050 (1125, 1200, 1275) (1350, 1425, 1500) (1575, 1650) m / 1149 (1230, 1312, 1393) (1476, 1557, 1640) (1721, 1803) yds of lace weight yarn.

Sample knitted with yarns

350 (375, 400, 425) (450, 475, 500) (525, 550) g of Sandnes Garn Kos (62% baby alpaca, 9% wool, 29% nylon – 150 m / 164 yds / 50 g) in the colour 2112 **together with** 90 (100, 110, 115) (120, 125, 130) (135, 140) g of Knitting for Olive Silk Mohair (70% mohair, 30% silk – 225 m / 246 yds / 25 g) in the colour Elderflower.

The yellow sample is worked holding one strand of alpaca and one strand of mohair together.

DIRECTIONS

The cardigan is worked flat beginning with the Upper Back while also shaping the shoulders. Stitches are picked up for the Upper Front separately, then all stitches are worked flat through the body. Stitches are picked up for the sleeves and worked in the round. Lastly stitches are picked up along the front edges for the button band. The final touch is knitting the pockets and attaching them to the cardigan.

Upper Back

Cast on 31 sts with the Backwards Loop Cast-On method with 5 mm / US 8 (80–100 cm / 32–40") circular needles. Start shaping the back and shoulders, placing removable stitch markers in the first and last st to mark where sts will be picked up later for the shoulder seams on the first row.

Work as follows:
Row 1 (RS): K1 and place removable stitch marker in this first st, k2, work row 1 of Chart A, k2, k1 and place removable stitch marker in this last st.
Row 2 (WS): P3, work row 2 of Chart A, p3. 2 sts increased.
Row 3: K3, work the next row of Chart A, k3. 2 sts increased.
Row 4: P3, work the next row of Chart A, p3. 2 sts increased.

There are 37 sts in total.

Continue in this manner, repeating rows 3–4, until all rows 1–18 of Chart A have been completed.

There are 65 sts in total.

Row 19 (RS): K3, M1L, PM, work row 1 of Chart B, PM, M1R, k3. 2 sts increased.
Row 20 (WS): P3, M1Rp, p1, SM, work row 2 of Chart B, SM, p1, M1Lp, p3. 2 sts increased.
Row 21: K3, M1L, k to m, SM, work the next row of Chart B, SM, k to last 3 sts, M1R, k3. 2 sts increased.
Row 22: P3, M1Rp, p to m, SM, work the next row of Chart B, SM, p to last 3 sts, M1Lp, p3. 2 sts increased.

There are 73 sts in total.

Continue in this manner, repeating rows 21–22, 6 (7, 8, 9) (10, 11, 12) (13, 14) more times, working through Chart B as many times as necessary.

There are 97 (101, 105, 109) (113, 117, 121) (125, 129) sts in total.

Shoulder shaping is complete. Place removable stitch markers in the first and last st to mark where sts will be picked up later for the shoulder seams.

Continue working the back without increases as follows:
Row 1 (RS): K19 (21, 23, 25) (27, 29, 31) (33, 35), SM, work row 5 (7, 9, 11) (1, 3, 5) (7, 9) of Chart B, SM, k19 (21, 23, 25) (27, 29, 31) (33, 35).
Row 2 (WS): P to m, SM, work row 6 (8, 10, 12) (2, 4, 6) (8, 10) of Chart B, SM, p to end.
Row 3: K to m, SM, work the next row of Chart B, SM, k to end.
Row 4: P to m, SM, work the next row of Chart B, SM, p to end.

Continue in this manner, repeating rows 3–4, for 8 (9, 12, 13) (13, 15, 16) (16, 18) more times, working through Chart B as many times as necessary. This means you'll work row 12 (4, 12, 4) (6, 12, 4) (6, 12) of Chart B on the last WS row.

Cut the yarn and place sts on hold while you work the Upper Front next, transferring the sts onto a stitch wire or some scrap yarn.

Right Upper Front

With 5 mm / US 8 needles, pick up and k31 (33, 35, 37) (39, 41, 43) (45, 47) sts, working from the right outer edge stitch marker to the right side stitch marker placed at the cast on edge (when looking at the piece with the RS facing you and the cast on edge facing up towards the top). You can remove these markers now.

Work one set-up row and place stitch markers to mark the pattern motif as follows:

Set-up row (WS): P2, PM, k1, p6, k1, p9, k1, p6, k1, PM, p4 (6, 8, 10) (12, 14, 16) (18, 20).

Start shaping the armhole as follows:
Row 1 (RS): K to m, SM, work row 1 of Chart C, SM, k2.
Row 2 (WS): P2, SM, work row 2 of Chart C, SM, p to end.
Row 3: K2, ssk, k to m, SM, work the next row of Chart C, SM, k2. 1 st decreased.
Row 4: P2, SM, work the next row of Chart C, SM, p to end.
Row 5: K to m, SM, work the next row of Chart C, SM, k2.
Row 6: P2, SM, work the next row of Chart C, SM, p to end.

There are 30 (32, 34, 36) (38, 40, 42) (44, 46) sts in total.

Continue in this manner, repeating rows 3–6, for 0 (1, 2, 3) (4, 5, 6) (7, 8) more times, working through Chart C as many times as necessary.

There are 30 (31, 32, 33) (34, 35, 36) (37, 38) sts in total.

Continue in your chosen size as follows:

Size XS
Row 7 (RS): K to m, SM, work row 7 of Chart C, SM, k2.
Row 8 (WS): P2, SM, work row 8 of Chart C, SM, p to end.
Row 9: K to m, SM, work the next row of Chart C, SM, k2.
Row 10: P2, SM, work the next row of Chart C, SM, p to end.
Rows 11–24: Continue in this manner, repeating rows 9–10, 7 more times, meaning you'll work row 12 of Chart C on the last WS row.

Size S
Row 11 (RS): K to m, SM, work row 11 of Chart C, SM, k2.
Row 12 (WS): P2, SM, work row 12 of Chart C, SM, p to end.
Row 13: K to m, SM, work the next row of Chart C, SM, k2.
Row 14: P2, SM, work the next row of Chart C, SM, p to end.
Rows 15–24: Continue in this manner, repeating rows 13–14, 5 more times, meaning you'll work row 12 of Chart C on the last WS row.

Sizes M (2XL, 5XL)
Row 15 (27, 39) (RS): K to m, SM, work row 3 of Chart C, SM, k2.
Row 16 (28, 40) (WS): P2, SM, work row 4 of Chart C, SM, p to end.
Row 17 (29, 41): K to m, SM, work the next row of Chart C, SM, k2.
Row 18 (30, 42): P2, SM, work the next row of Chart C, SM, p to end.
Rows 19–24 (31– 36, 42–48): Continue in this manner, repeating rows 17–18, 29–30, 41–42, 3 more times, meaning you'll work row 12 of Chart C on the last WS row.

Sizes L (3XL)
Row 19 (31) (RS): K to m, SM, work row 7 of Chart C, SM, k2.
Row 20 (32) (WS): P2, SM, work row 8 of Chart C, SM, p to end.

Row 21 (33): K to m, SM, work row 9 of Chart C, SM, k2.
Row 22 (34): P2, SM, work row 10 of Chart C, SM, p to end.
Row 23 (35): K to m, SM, work row 11 of Chart C, SM, k2.
Row 24 (36): P2, SM, work row 12 of Chart C, SM, p to end.

Sizes XL (4XL)
Row 32 (35) (RS): K to m, SM, work row 11 of Chart C, SM, k2.
Row 33 (36) (WS): P2, SM, work row 12 of Chart C, SM, p to end.

All sizes
Next, begin shaping the front neckline as follows:

Row 1 (RS): K to m, SM, work row 1 of Chart C, SM, M1R, k to end. 1 st increased.
Row 2 (WS): P to m, SM, work row 2 of Chart C, SM, p to end.
Row 3: K to m, SM, work row 3 of Chart C, SM, k to end.
Row 4: P to m, SM, work row 4 of Chart C, SM, p to end.

There are 31 (32, 33, 34) (35, 36, 37) (38, 39) sts in total.

Row 5 (RS): K to m, SM, work the next row of Chart C, SM, k to last 2 sts, M1R, k to end. 1 st increased.
Row 6 (WS): P to m, SM, work the next row of Chart C, SM, p to end.
Row 7: K to m, SM, work the next row of Chart C, SM, k to end.
Row 8: P to m, SM, work the next row of Chart C, SM, p to end.

There are 30 (31, 32, 33) (34, 35, 36) (37, 38) sts in total.

Repeat rows 5–8, for 4 (5, 7, 8) (8, 7, 8) (8, 7) more times, meaning you'll work row 12 (4, 12, 4) (4, 12, 4) (4, 12) of Chart C on the last WS row.

There are 36 (38, 41, 43) (44, 44, 46) (46, 47) sts in total.

Only sizes XL, 4XL
Work 2 more rows as follows:
Row 41 (RS): K to m, SM, work row 5 of Chart C, SM, k to end.
Row 42 (WS): P to m, SM, work row 6 of Chart C, SM, p to end.

All sizes
Cut the yarn and place the sts on hold while you work the Left Upper Front.

Left Upper Front

With 5 mm / US 8 needles, pick up and k31 (33, 35, 37) (39, 41, 43) (45, 47) sts, working from left neckline marker to the left outer edge stitch marker (when looking at the piece with the RS facing you and the cast-on edge facing up towards the top). You can remove these markers now.

Work one set-up row and place stitch markers to mark the pattern motif as follows:

Set-up row (WS): P4 (6, 8, 10) (12, 14, 16) (18, 20), PM, k1, p6, k1, p9, k1, p6, k1, PM, p2.

Start shaping the armhole as follows:
Row 1 (RS): K2, SM, work row 1 of Chart C, SM, k to end.
Row 2 (WS): P to m, SM, work row 2 of Chart C, SM, p2.
Row 3: K2, SM, work the next row of Chart C, SM, k to last 4 sts, k2tog, k2. 1 st decreased.
Row 4: P to m, SM, work the next row of Chart C, SM, p2.
Row 5: K2, SM, work the next row of Chart C, SM, k to end.
Row 6: P to m, SM, work the next row of Chart C, SM, p2.

There are 30 (32, 34, 36) (38, 40, 42) (43, 46) sts in total.

Continue in this manner, repeating rows 3–6, 0 (1, 2, 3) (4, 5, 6) (7, 8) more times, working through Chart C as many times as necessary.

There are 30 (31, 32, 33) (34, 35, 36) (37, 38) sts in total.

Continue in your chosen size as follows:

Size XS
Row 7 (RS): K2, SM, work row 7 of Chart C, SM, k to end.
Row 8 (WS): P to m, SM, work row 8 of Chart C, SM, p2.
Row 9: K2, SM, work the next row of Chart C, SM, k to end.
Row 10: P to m, SM, work the next row of Chart C, SM, p2.
Rows 11–24: Continue in this manner, repeating rows 9–10, 7 more times, meaning you'll work row 12 of Chart C on the last WS row.

Size S
Row 11 (RS): K2, SM, work row 11 of Chart C, SM, k to end.
Row 12 (WS): P to m, SM, work row 12 of Chart C, SM, p2.
Row 13: K2, SM, work the next row of Chart C, SM, k to end.
Row 14: P to m, SM, work the next row of Chart C, SM, p2.
Rows 15–24: Continue in this manner, repeating rows 13–14, 5 more times, meaning you'll work row 12 of Chart C on the last WS row.

Sizes M (2XL, 5XL)
Row 15 (27, 39) (RS): K2, SM, work row 3 of Chart C, SM, k to end.
Row 16 (28, 40) (WS): P to m, SM, work row 4 of Chart C, SM, p2.
Row 17 (29, 41): K2, SM, work the next row of Chart C, SM, k to end.
Row 18 (30, 42): P to m, SM, work the next row of Chart C, SM, p2.
Rows 19–24, 31– 36, 42–48: Continue in this manner, repeating rows 17–18, 29–30, 41–42, 3 more times, meaning you'll work row 12 of Chart C on the last WS row.

Sizes L (3XL)
Row 19 (31) (RS): K2, SM, work row 7 of Chart C, SM, k to end.
Row 20 (32) (WS): P to m, SM, work row 8 of Chart C, SM, p2.
Row 21 (33): K2, SM, work row 9 of Chart C, SM, k to end.
Row 22 (34): P to m, SM, work row 10 of Chart C, SM, p2.
Row 23 (35): K2, SM, work row 11 of Chart C, SM, k to end.
Row 24 (36): P to m, SM, work row 12 of Chart C, SM, p2.

Sizes XL (4XL)
Row 32 (35) (RS): K2, SM, work row 11 of Chart C, SM, k to end.
Row 33 (36) (WS): P to m, SM, work row 12 of Chart C, SM, p2.

All sizes
Next start shaping the front neckline as follows:
Row 1 (RS): K2, M1L, SM, work row 1 of Chart C, SM, k to end. 1 st increased.
Row 2 (WS): P to m, SM, work row 2 of Chart C, SM, p to end.
Row 3: K to m, SM, work row 3 of Chart C to m, SM, k to end.
Row 4: P to m, SM, work row 4 of Chart C, SM, p to end.

There are 31 (32, 33, 34) (35, 36, 37) (38, 39) sts in total.

Row 5 (RS): K2, M1L, k to m, SM, work the next row of Chart C to m, SM, k to end. 1 st increased.
Row 6 (WS): P to m, SM, work the next row of Chart C, SM, p to end.

Row 7: K to m, SM, work the next row of Chart C, SM, k to end.
Row 8: P to m, SM, work the next row of Chart C, SM, p to end.

There are 32 (33, 34, 35) (36, 37, 38) (39, 40) sts in total.

Repeat rows 5–8, for 4 (5, 7, 8) (8, 7, 8) (8, 7) more times, meaning you'll work row 12 (4, 12, 4) (4, 12, 4) (4, 12) of Chart C on the last WS row.

There are 36 (38, 41, 43) (44, 45, 46) (47, 47) sts in total.

Only sizes XL, 4XL
Work 2 more rows as follows:
Row 41 (RS): K to m, SM, work row 5 of Chart C, SM, k to end.
Row 42 (WS): P to m, SM, work row 6 of Chart C, SM, p to end.

All sizes
Don't cut the yarn yet. Next, we'll join everything on the same circular needle for the body.

Body

Join the Left and Right Front sts together with the Upper Back sts to work the body in the rnd. Additional sts will be cast on for the underarms on the first row.

Joining row 1 (RS):
Left Front sts: K to m, SM, work row 1 (5, 1, 5) (7, 1, 5) (7, 1) of Chart C, SM, k to end of Left Front sts, cast on 2 (4, 6, 8) (10, 12, 12) (14, 16) sts with the Backwards Loop Cast-On method for the underarm sts,
Upper Back sts: k to m, SM, work row 1 (5, 1, 5) (7, 1, 5) (7, 1) of Chart B, SM, k to end of Upper Back sts, cast on 2 (4, 6, 8) (10, 12, 12) (14, 16) sts for the underarm sts,
Right Front sts: k to m, SM, work row 1 (5, 1, 5) (7, 1, 5) (7, 1) of Chart C, SM, k to end.

There are 173 (185, 199, 211) (221, 231, 237) (247, 255) sts in total.

Row 2 (WS): P to m, SM, work row 2 (6, 2, 6) (8, 2, 6) (8, 2) of Chart C, SM, p to m, SM, work row 2 (6, 2, 6) (8, 2, 6) (8, 2) of Chart B, SM, p to m, SM, work row 2 (6, 2, 6) (8, 2, 6) (8, 2) of Chart C, SM, p to end.
Row 3: K to m, SM, work the next row of Chart C, SM, k to m, SM, work the next row of Chart B, SM, k to m, SM, work the next row of Chart C, SM, k to end.
Row 4: P to m, SM, work the next row of Chart C, SM, p to m, SM, work the next row of Chart B, SM, p to m, SM, work the next row of Chart C, SM, p to end.

Continue working in this manner, repeating rows 3–4, 4 (2, 4, 2) (1, 4, 2) (1, 4) more times, meaning you'll work the remaining rows 5–12 (9–12, 5–12, 9–12) (11–12, 5–12, 9–12) (11–12, 5–12) of Chart C and B.

Then continue working the body in the same manner, repeating rows 3–4 until you've completed all rows 1–12 of Chart C and B a total of 4 (5, 5, 6) (6, 6, 7) (7, 7) times (or until the body measures 4 cm / 1.5" less than total desired length).

Change to 3 mm / US 2.5 circular needles and work the rib hem as follows:

Row 1 (RS): K2, *p1, k1* to last 3 sts, p1, k2.
Row 2 (WS): P2, *k1, p1* to last 3 sts, k1, p2.

Repeat rows 1–2 until rib hem measures 4 cm / 1.5" in length.

Bind off using the Standard Bind-Off method (or your preferred bind-off method).

Sleeves

The sleeve sts are picked up and k in the rnd along the armhole openings, using either 5 mm / US 8 (40–60 cm / 16–24") circular needles, DPNs or longer circular needles for the Magic Loop technique.

Work as follows:
With the RS facing, pick up and k54 (54, 64, 64) (74, 74, 84) (84, 94) sts evenly around the armhole opening starting from the middle of the underarm. Join to work in the rnd and place a marker to mark the beginning of rnd.

Rnd 1: K15 (15, 20, 20) (25, 25, 30) (30, 35), PM, work rnd 1 of Chart C, PM, k to end.
Rnd 2: K to m, SM, work rnd 2 of Chart C, SM, k to end.
Rnd 3: K to m, SM, work the next rnd of Chart C, SM, k to end.
Rnds 4–12: Continue in this manner, repeating rnd 3 until all rnds 1–12 of Chart C are completed.

Rnd 13 (dec rnd): K1, k2tog, k to m, SM, work rnd 1 of Chart C, SM, k to last 3 sts, ssk, k1. 2 sts decreased.
Rnds 14–24: K to m, SM, work the next rnd of Chart C, SM, k to end.

There are 52 (52, 62, 62) (72, 72, 82) (82, 92) sts in total.

Continue in this manner, repeating rnds 13–2, 5 more times (or until the sleeve measures 4 cm / 1.5" less than total desired length).

There are 42 (42, 52, 52) (62, 62, 72) (72, 82) sts in total.

Change to 3 mm / US 2.5 needles and work *k1, p1* rib until the cuff measures 4 cm / 1.5" in total.

Bind off using the Standard Bind-Off method (or your preferred Bind-Off method).

Work the other sleeve the same way.

Button band

For the button band, sts are picked up along the entire Left and Right Front and the Upper Back neck cast on edge with 3 mm / US 2.5 circular needles. The button band is worked in 1 x 1 rib flat and 5 buttonholes are worked along the Left Front edge.

With 3 mm / US 2.5 circular needles (80–100 cm / 32–40") or longer, pick up and k233 (243, 243, 253) (253, 253, 253) (253, 253) sts evenly along the complete edge of the cardigan (**Note**! if your cardigan is longer or shorter: pick up fewer or more sts on either side, keeping the distribution rate at approximately 5 sts per every 7 rows).

Begin picking up sts at the bottom of the left side (when looking at the cardigan from the front, RS facing you), continue along the back neck, and down to the end of the right side. If necessary, you can also use two circular needles for this. The rate for picking up sts along both front edges is approx. 5 sts per 7 rows/sts (in other words: pick up and k every st for 2 rows/sts, skip 1, pick up and k every sts for 3 rows/sts, skip 1) and the pickup rate for the back neck is 1 st per 1 st.

Work the button band as follows:
Row 1 (WS): P2, *k1, p1* to last st, p1.
Row 2 (RS): K2, *p1, k1* to last st, k1.
Row 3 (WS): P2, *k1, p1* to last st, p1.

Place 5 removable stitch markers to mark where the buttonholes will be worked along the left front edge of the cardigan (when looking at the cardigan from the front, RS facing you). The buttonholes are worked over 3 sts (starting with a p st) by binding off sts on one row and then casting on new sts on the following row.

Place the bottom buttonhole 2 sts from the bottom edge of the hem, and place the top buttonhole at the place where the neckline shaping ends. Spread out the 3 remaining buttonholes at an even distance between each other between the top and bottom buttonhole.

Row 4 (RS): K2, [work buttonhole as follows: p1, k1, pull first st over second st, p1, pull first st over second st, k1, *p1, k1* to the next buttonhole m] 4 times, work the top buttonhole and then continue *k1, p1* to the last 2 sts, k2.
Row 5 (WS): P2, *k1, p1* to the top buttonhole, [cast on 2 sts with the Backwards-Loop cast- on method at the buttonhole, *p1, k1* to the next buttonhole] 4 times, cast on 2 sts for the last buttonhole, p2.
Row 6: K2, *p1, k1* to last st, k1.
Row 7: P2, *k1, p1* to last st, p1.

Bind off all sts using the Standard Bind-Off method.

Pockets

Two pockets are worked separately flat and attached to the cardigan by hand sewing.

Cast on 27 sts for 1 × 1 rib with the Long Tail Cast-On method on 3 mm / US 2.5 circular needles (start with a p st).

Row 1 (RS): K1, *p1, k1* to end of row.
Row 2 (WS): Sl1 wyif, *k1, p1* to end of row.
Rows 3, 5, 7: Sl1 wyib, *p1, k1* to end of row.
Rows 4, 6, 8: Sl1 wyif, *k1, p1* to end of row.

Change to 5 mm / US 8 needles and continue as follows:

Row 1 (RS): Sl1 wyib, work row 1 of Chart C, k1.
Row 2 (WS): Sl1 wyif, work row 2 of Chart C, p1.
Row 3: Sl1 wyib, work the next row of Chart C, k1.
Row 4: Sl1 wyif, work the next row of Chart C, p1.
Rows 5–24: Repeat rows 3–4, until all rows 1–12 of Chart C are completed twice.
Row 25 (RS): Sl1 wyib, work row 1 of Chart C, k1.
Row 26 (WS): Sl1 wyif, work row 2 of Chart C, p1.

Bind off using the Standard Bind-Off method.

Work the other pocket the same way.

Finishing

Weave in all ends. Attach the pockets by hand sewing on each front. Place the bottom edge of the pocket just at the edge of the hem rib so that it aligns with the lace motif of the cardigan.

Start by sewing the bottom side of the pocket onto the cardigan with the top stitch, and then sew the two sides onto the cardigan with the mattress stitch (invisible stitch). You can gently steam block the pocket seams by placing a damp kitchen cloth onto the fabric and use a hot iron to create steam that will allow the stitches to relax and even out.

Spread out the buttons along the right front edge (when looking at the cardigan in front of you with the RS facing up) so that they correspond with the button-holes on the left side. Attach them by hand sewing.

CHART A

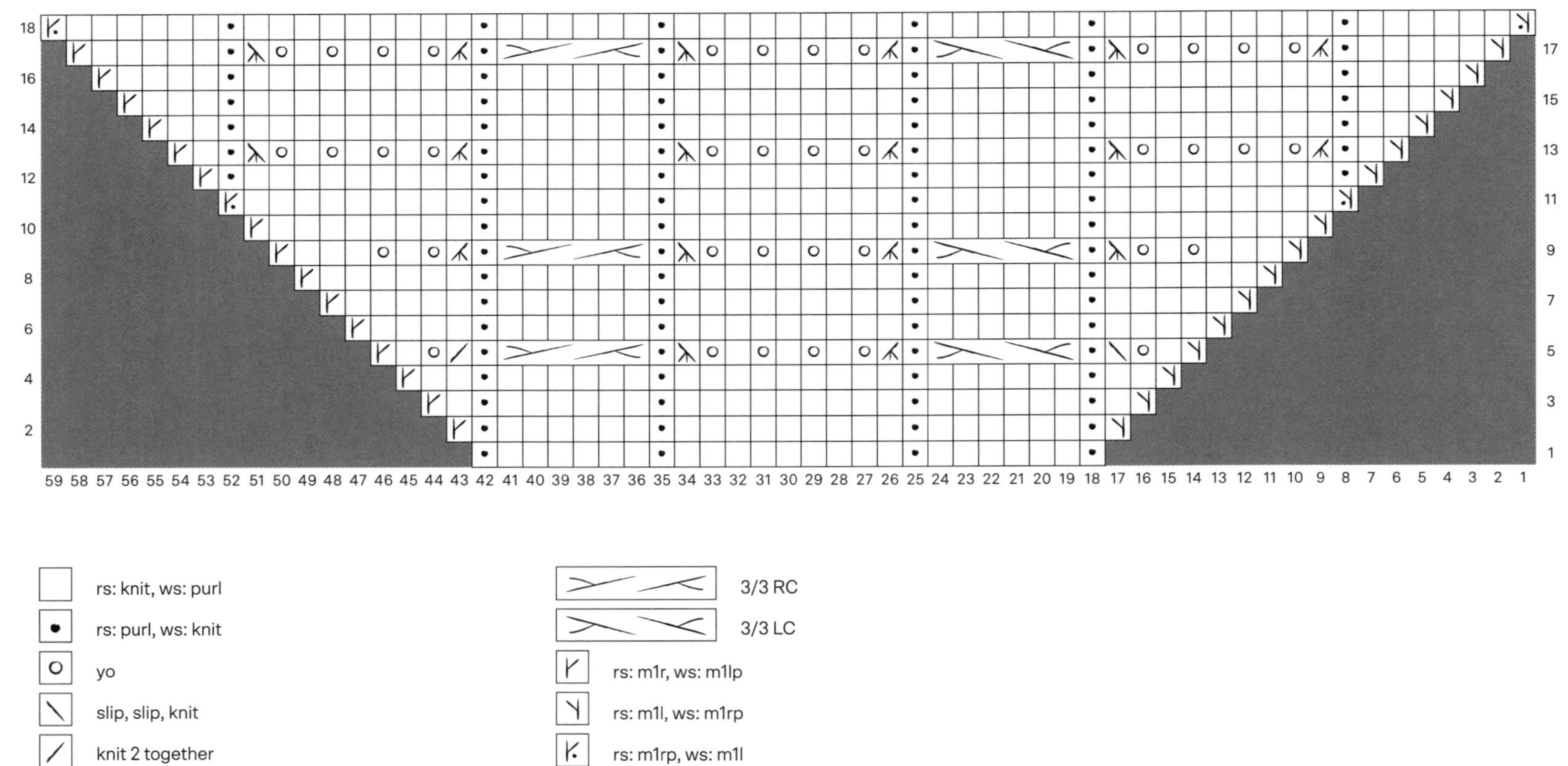

- rs: knit, ws: purl
- rs: purl, ws: knit
- yo
- slip, slip, knit
- knit 2 together
- rs: knit 3 together
- rs: slip, slip, slip, knit
- 3/3 RC
- 3/3 LC
- rs: m1r, ws: m1lp
- rs: m1l, ws: m1rp
- rs: m1rp, ws: m1l
- rs: m1lp, ws: m1r
- no stitch

CHART B

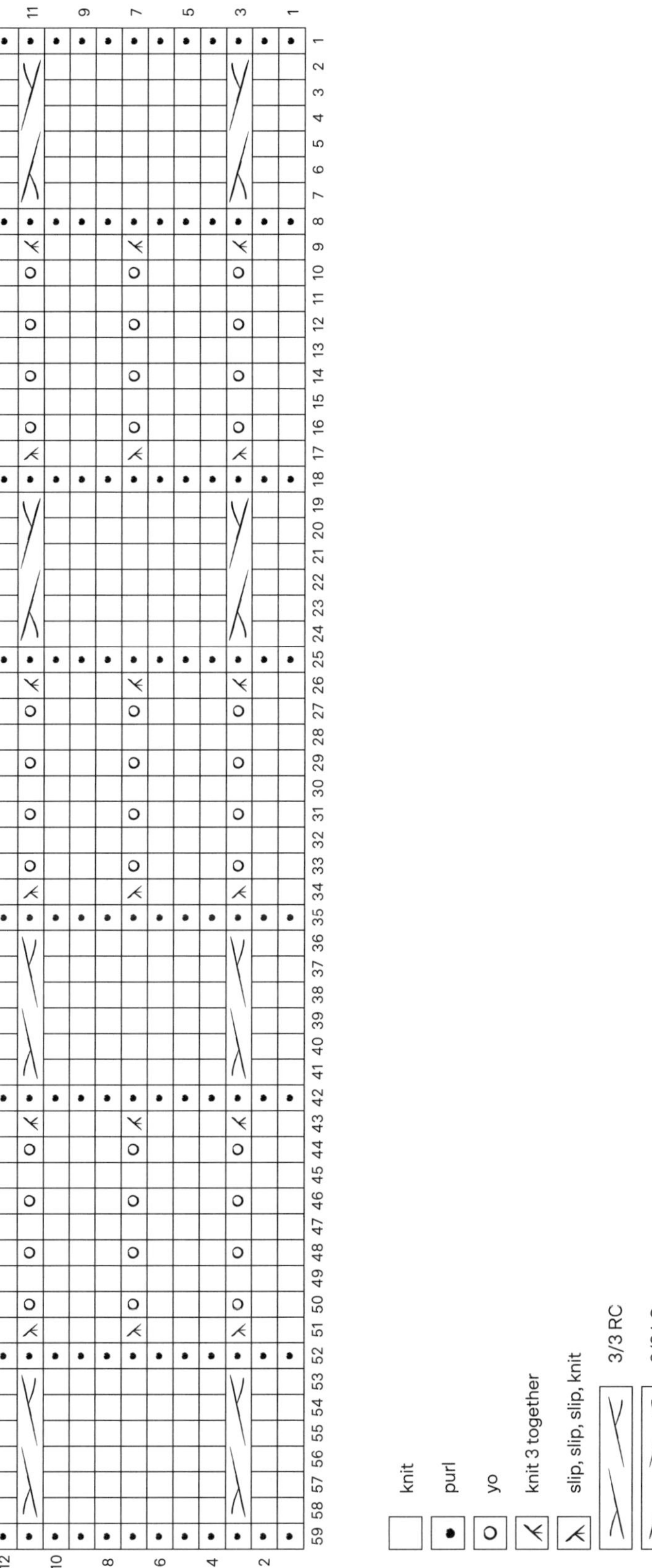

- knit
- purl
- yo
- knit 3 together
- slip, slip, slip, knit
- 3/3 RC
- 3/3 LC

CHART C

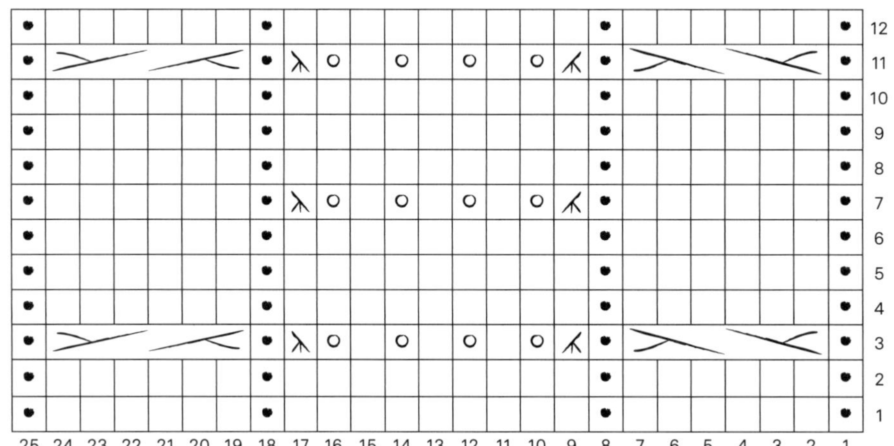

knit

purl

yo

knit 3 together

slip, slip, slip, knit

3/3 RC

3/3 LC

STYLING TIP #8

Create a stylish contrast by pairing a soft, cosy cardigan with a crisp white poplin shirt for a look that's both fresh and modern.

Time for a break? Just throw on the Coffee Run sweater, and you'll look stylish when popping to the nearby cafe for a snack! This modern raglan-style sweater has a relaxed, slightly cropped fit with narrow sleeves for a flattering silhouette. The key characteristics are the twisted rib details around the raglan and underarm seams, adding a smart touch to the garment. You'll breeze through the pattern thanks to the airy fabric in Stockinette stitch created with large needles.

COFFEE RUN

OYSHO

Sizes

XS (S, M, L) (XL, 2XL, 3XL) (4XL, 5XL)

Finished garment measurements

Bust circumference: 91 (100, 111, 120) (131, 140, 149) (160, 169) cm / 35.75 (39.25, 43.75, 47.25) (51.5, 55, 58.75) (63, 66.5)".

Length from underarm to hem:
35 cm / 13.75" all sizes (or desired length).

Sleeve length from underarm to hem:
50 cm /19.75" (or desired length).

Upper sleeve circumference:
31 (34.5, 40, 44.5) (50, 54.5, 59) (64.5, 69) cm / 12.25 (13.5, 15.75, 17.5) (19.75, 21.5, 23.25) (25.5, 27.25)".

Cuff circumference: 21 (24, 27, 30) (30, 32, 33) (38, 41) cm / 8.25 (9.5, 10.75, 11.75) (11.75, 12.5, 13) (15, 16.25)".

The Coffee Run sweater is designed to have about 10–15 cm / 4–6" positive ease for a relaxed fit.

Sample shown in size S (Kika has a bust of approx. 89 cm / 35").

Gauge

18 sts × 25 rows/rnds = 10 cm / 4" in Stockinette st on 5 mm / US 8 needles, after blocking.

20 sts × 30 rows/rnds = 10 cm / 4" in *k1 tbl, p1* rib on 3 mm / US 2.5 needles, after blocking.

Needles

3 mm / US 2.5: circular needles 40–60 cm / 16–24" for neck opening and 80–100 cm / 32–40" for hem rib, and DPNs for sleeve rib (or use the Magic Loop technique).

5 mm / US 8: circular needles 80–100 cm / 32–40" for body, and circular needles 40 cm / 16" for sleeves or DPNs (or use the Magic Loop technique).

Notions

9 stitch markers, tapestry needle, stitch holder or scrap yarn.

Suggested yarn

The sweater is worked with one strand of fingering weight yarn held together with two strands of lace weight yarn to produce a drapey and light fabric.

You need approx. 800 (860, 900, 1000) (1060, 1100, 1200) (1300, 1400) m / 875 (941, 984, 1094) (1159, 1203, 1312) (1422, 1531) yds of fingering weight yarn **together with** 800 (860, 900, 1000) (1060, 1100, 1200) (1300, 1400) m / 875 (941, 984, 1094) (1159, 1203, 1312) (1422, 1531) yds lace weight yarn **together with** 800 (860, 900, 1000) (1060, 1100, 1200) (1300, 1400) m / 875 (941, 984, 1094) (1159, 1203, 1312) (1422, 1531) yds lace weight yarn.

Sample knitted with yarns

200 (215, 225, 250) (265, 275, 300) (325, 350) g of Filcolana Arwetta (80% wool, 20% nylon – 210 m / 230 yds / 50 g) in the colour 954 **together with** 115 (125, 130, 145) (150, 155, 170) (185, 200) g of Filcolana Alva (100% alpaca – 175 m / 191 yds / 25 g) in the colour 401 **together with** 70 (75, 80, 85) (90, 95, 100) (110, 120) g of Krea Deluxe

deluxe Silk Mohair (45% silk, 33% mohair, 22% alpaca – 240 m / 262 yds / 20 g) in the colour 51.

The sweater is worked by holding three strands together.

DIRECTIONS

The sweater is worked top down seamlessly. The neckline is shaped by working German short rows to guarantee a comfortable and stylish fit. The sleeves are knitted extra long for a feminine and cosy look. The collar, hem and sleeve cuffs are worked in a twisted rib for a polished finishing touch.

Collar

Cast on 92 (100, 100, 100) (100, 100, 100) (108, 108) sts with the Long-Tail Cast-On method (or your preferred elastic cast-on method) with 3 mm / US 2.5 (40–60 cm / 16–24) circular needles and join to work in the rnd. Place marker to indicate BOR-m.

Work *k1 tbl, p1* rib until collar measures 3.5 cm / 1.5".

Yoke

The yoke is shaped by working increases on every second rnd on each side of the four raglan seams, and the neckline is shaped by working German Short Rows flat.

Change to 5 mm / US 8 circular needles and place 8 markers on the first set-up rnd to mark where the raglan seams will be.

Tip! You can use a pair of different coloured stitch markers for each raglan seam and the BOR-m to stay organised (the BOR-m is in the middle of the back).

Set-up rnd: K13 (13, 13, 13) (13, 13, 13) (14, 14) (= half of back sts), PM1, p1, *k1 tbl, p1* 3 times (= raglan seam), PM2, k 7 (9, 9, 9) (9, 9, 9) (11, 11) (= sleeve sts), PM3, p1, *k1 tbl, p1* 3 times (= raglan seam), PM4, k 25 (27, 27, 27) (27, 27, 27) (29, 29) (=front sts), PM5, p1, *k1 tbl, p1* 3 times (= raglan seam), PM6, k 7 (9, 9, 9) (9, 9, 9) (11, 11) (= sleeve sts), PM7, p1, *k1 tbl, p1* 3 times (= raglan seam), PM8, k 12 (14, 14, 14) (14, 14, 14) (15, 15) (= half of back sts).

Next, German short rows are worked flat to shape the back of the neck so that it is higher than the front while at the same time starting to work the increases for the raglan shaping.

German short row 1 (RS): K to 1 st before m (= half of back sts), M1R, k1, SM1, p1, *k1 tbl, p1* 3 times (= raglan seam), SM2, k1, M1L, k to 1 st before m (= sleeve sts), M1R, k1, SM3, p1, *k1 tbl, p1* 3 times (= raglan seam), SM4, k1, M1L, k1 (= front sts). Turn work. 4 sts increased.

German short row 2 (WS): Make double stitch, p to m, SM4, k1, *p1 tbl, k1* 3 times (= raglan seam), SM3, p to m (= sleeve sts), SM2, k1, *p1 tbl, k1* 3 times (= raglan seam), SM1, p to BOR-m, SM, p to 1 st before m (= half of back sts), M1Lp, p1, SM8, k1, *p1 tbl, k1* 3 times (= raglan seam), SM7, p1, M1Rp, p to 1 st before m (= sleeve sts), M1Lp, p1, SM6, k1, *p1 tbl, k1* 3 times (= raglan seam), SM5, p1, M1Rp, p1 (= front sts). Turn work. 4 sts increased.

German short row 3 (RS): Make double stitch, k to m, SM5, p1, *k1 tbl, p1* 3 times, SM6, k to m, SM7, p1, *k1 tbl, p1* 3 times, SM8, k to BOR-m, SM, k to 1 st before m (= half of back sts), M1R, k1, SM1, p1, *k1 tbl, p1* 3 times, SM2, k1, M1L, k to 1 st before m (= sleeve sts), M1R, k1, SM3, p1, *k1 tbl, p1* 3 times, SM4, k1, M1L, k1, k double stitch, k1 (= front sts). Turn work. 4 sts increased.

German short row 4 (WS): Make double stitch, p to m, SM4, k1, *p1 tbl, k1* 3 times, SM3, p to m (= sleeve sts), SM2, k1, *p1 tbl, k1* 3 times, SM1, p to BOR-m, SM, p to 1 st before m (= half of back sts), M1Lp, p1, SM8, k1, *p1 tbl, k1* 3 times, SM7, p1, M1Rp, p to 1 st before m (= sleeve sts), M1Lp, p1, SM6, k1, *p1 tbl, k1* 3 times, SM5, p1, M1Rp, p1, p double stitch, p1 (= front sts). Turn work. 4 sts increased.

German short row 5 (RS): Make double stitch, k to m, SM5, p1, *k1 tbl, p1* 3 times, SM6, k to m, SM7, p1, *k1 tbl, p1* 3 times, SM8, k to BOR-m, SM, k to 1 st before m (= half of back sts), M1R, k1, SM1, p1, *k1 tbl, p1* 3 times, SM2, k1, M1L, k to 1 st before m (= sleeve sts), M1R, k1, SM3, p1, *k1 tbl, p1* 3 times, SM4, k1, M1L, k to double st, k double stitch, k1 (= front sts). Turn work. 4 sts increased.

German short row 6 (WS): Make double stitch, p to m, SM4, k1, *p1 tbl, k1* 3 times, SM3, p to m (= sleeve sts), SM2, k1, *p1 tbl, k1* 3 times, SM1, p to BOR-m, SM, p to 1 st before m (= half of back sts), M1Lp, p1, SM8, k1, *p1 tbl, k1* 3 times, SM7, p1, M1Rp, p to 1 st before m (= sleeve sts), M1Lp, p1, SM6, k1, *p1 tbl, k1* 3 times, SM5, p1, M1Rp, p to double st, p double stitch, p1 (= front sts). Turn work. 4 sts increased.

German short rows 7–12: Repeat rows 5–6 for 3 more times.

German short row 13 (RS): Make double stitch, k to m, SM5, p1, *k1 tbl, p1* 3 times, SM6, k to m, SM7, p1, *k1 tbl, p1* 3 times, SM8, k to BOR-m.

German Short Rows are now complete.

There are 140 (148, 148, 148) (148, 148, 148) (156, 156) sts in total for the yoke (**note**: count the remaining two double sts as one st each). Front and back: 37 (39, 39, 39) (39, 39, 39) (41, 41) sts for each Front and Back. Sleeves: 19 (21, 21, 21) (21, 21, 21) (23, 23) sts. Raglan seams: 7 sts for each raglan seam (4 seams in total).

Continue working the yoke in the rnd while working increases for the raglan shaping as follows (k both the double stitches as normal k sts on the first rnd):

Rnd 1: K to 1 st before m (= half of back sts), M1R, k1, SM1, p1, *k1 tbl, p1* 3 times, SM2, k1, M1L, k to 1 st before m (= sleeve sts), M1R, k1, SM3, p1, *k1 tbl, p1* 3 times, SM4, k1, M1L, k to 1 st before m (= front sts), M1R, k1, SM5, p1, *k1 tbl, p1* 3 times, SM6, k1, M1L, k to 1 st before m (= sleeve sts), M1R, k1, SM7, p1, *k1 tbl, p1* 3 times, SM8, k1, M1L, k to BOR-m. 8 sts increased.

There are 148 (156, 156, 156) (156, 156, 156) (164, 164) sts in total.

Rnd 2: K to m, SM1, p1, *k1 tbl, p1* 3 times, SM2, k to m, SM3, p1, *k1 tbl, p1* 3 times (= raglan seam), SM4, k to m, SM5, p1, *k1 tbl, p1* 3 times (= raglan seam), SM6, k to m, SM7, p1, *k1 tbl, p1* 3 times (= raglan seam), SM8, k to BOR-m.

Repeat Rnds 1–2, 13 (14, 19, 23) (28, 32, 36) (39, 43) more times.

There are 252 (268, 308, 340) (380, 412, 444) (476, 508) sts in total. Front and back: 65 (69, 79, 87) (97, 105, 113) (121, 129) sts. Sleeves: 47 (51, 61, 69) (79, 87, 95) (103, 111) sts. Raglan seams: 7 sts each raglan seam (4 seams in total).

Only sizes XS (S, M)
Repeat rnd 2, 8 (10, 10) more times.

Tip! I recommend trying on the sweater at this point to make sure it fits the way you prefer. If the yoke feels too short, repeat rnd 2 as many times as necessary for additional yoke length.

Body

Next, we're going to knit the body and put the sts for the sleeves on hold.

Continue like this:
K to m (= half of back sts), SM1, p1, *k1 tbl, p1* 3 times, RM2, transfer 47 (51, 61, 69) (79, 87, 95) (103, 111) sleeve sts onto a holder (for example a stitch holder or a piece of scrap yarn), cast on 5 (7, 7, 7) (7, 7, 7) (9, 9) sts for underarm with the Backwards Loop Cast-On method, RM3, p1, *k1 tbl, p1* 3 times, SM4, k to m (= front sts), SM5, p1, *k1 tbl, p1* 3 times, RM6, transfer 47 (51, 61, 69) (79, 87, 95) (103, 111) sleeve sts onto a holder, cast on 5 (7, 7, 7) (7, 7, 7) (9, 9) sts for underarm with the Backwards Loop Cast-On method, RM7, p1, *k1 tbl, p1* 3 times, SM8, k to BOR-m (= half of back sts).

There are 164 (180, 200, 216) (236, 252, 268) (288, 304) sts in total.

Rnd 1: [K to m, SM, p1, *k1 tbl, p1* 8 (10, 10, 10) (10, 10 10) (11, 11) times, SM] twice, k to BOR-m.

Repeat rnd 1 until the body measures 30 cm / 11.75" from the underarm (or until 5 cm / 2" less than desired total length).

Change to 3 mm / US 2.5 circular needles and work *k1 tbl, p1* rib until the hem measures 5 cm / 2".

Bind off using the Italian Bind-Off method (or your preferred bind-off method).

Sleeves

Transfer 47 (51, 61, 69) (79, 87, 95) (103, 111) sleeve sts that you had on hold onto 5 mm / US 8 40–60 cm / 16–24" circular needles, DPNs or longer circular needles for the Magic Loop technique.

Starting from the middle of underarm, pick up and k 2 (3, 3, 3) (3, 3, 3) (4, 4) sts from the underarm, k2 from the gap between the underarm and sleeve sts, k 47 (51, 61, 69) (79, 87, 95) (103, 111) sleeve sts, k2 from the gap between the sleeve sts and underarm, pick up and k 3 (4, 4, 4) (4, 4, 4) (5, 5) sts. Place marker to indicate BOR-m.

There are 56 (62, 72, 80) (90, 98, 106) (116, 124) sts in total for the sleeve.

Work in Stockinette st in the rnd until the sleeve measures 5 cm / 2" from the underarm.

Then work one dec rnd as follows:
Dec rnd: K1, k2tog, k to last 3 sts before m, ssk, k1. 2 sts decreased.

There are 54 (60, 70, 78) (88, 96, 104) (114, 122) sleeve sts in total.

Work in Stockinette st until the sleeve measures 45 cm / 17.75" (or, until sleeve measures 5 cm / 2" less than desired length) from the underarm **while at the same time** working Dec rnd approx. 10 (6.5, 5.5, 5.5) (5, 5, 4) (4.5, 4.5) cm / 4 (2.5, 2.25, 2.25) (2, 2, 1.5) (1.75, 1.75)" apart 3 (4, 6, 7) (7, 7, 9) (8, 8) more times.

Tip! Try on the sweater at this point to make sure you get a sleeve length that fits your preferences.

There are 48 (52, 58, 64) (74, 82, 86) (98, 106) sleeve sts in total.

Only sizes XL–5XL
Size XL: K4, *k2tog, k5* to end of rnd.
10 sts decreased.
Size 2XL: K2, *k6, k2tog* to end of rnd.
10 sts decreased.
Size 3XL: K2, *k5, k2tog* to end of rnd.
12 sts decreased.
Size 4XL: K2, *k6, k2tog* to end of rnd.
12 sts decreased.
Size 5XL: K6, *k3, k2tog* to end of rnd.
20 sts decreased.

There are 48 (52, 58, 64) (64, 72, 74) (86, 86) sleeve sts in total.

Change to 3 mm / US 2.5 (80–100 cm / 32–40") circular needles for the cuff and work in *k1 tbl, p1* rib until cuff measures 5 cm / 2".

Bind off using the Italian Bind-Off method (or your preferred stretchy bind-off method).

Finishing

Weave in all ends.

STYLING TIP #9

Layer your knitted sweater over a shirt to instantly add personality and flair to your outfit. The subtle glimpse of these details brings depth and a polished touch to your look. It's a simple trick that transforms an everyday sweater into a chic, layered ensemble.

With dropped shoulders and a wide neckline, this relaxed cardigan has an oversized fit that makes Daily Stripes both cosy and easy to wear. If you're not a fan of the purl stitch but would like to add a cardigan to your handmade wardrobe, this garter stitch design might be just the project for you! The body is worked flat, knitting every row, and the garter stitch stripes add an interesting structure to the piece – plus, they're quick to knit!

DAILY STRIPES

the gentlewoman

Sizes

XS (S, M, L) (XL, 2XL, 3XL) (4XL, 5XL)

Finished garment measurements

Bust circumference (including front edge placket): 95.5 (111.5, 122, 137) (147, 158, 163) (172, 178) cm / 37.5 (44, 48, 54) (58, 62.25, 64) (67.75, 70)".

Length from underarm to hem: 30 (31, 32, 32) (33, 33, 34) (35, 35) cm/ 12 (12.25, 12.5, 12.5) (13, 13, 13.5) (13.75, 13.75)".

Sleeve length from underarm to hem: 47 cm / 18.5" (or desired length).

Upper sleeve circumference: 36 (39, 40, 42.5) (45, 46, 47.5) (49, 50) cm / 14 (15.5, 15.75, 16.75) (17.75, 18, 18.75) (19.25, 19.75)".

Cuff circumference: 32 (34.5, 35.5, 37.5) (40, 41, 42) (43.5, 44.5) cm / 12.5 (13.5, 14, 14.75) (15.75, 16, 16.5) (17, 17.5)".

The Daily Stripes cardigan is designed to have about 20–30 cm / 8–12" positive ease for a relaxed and oversized fit.

Sample shown in size M (Kika has a bust of approx. 89 cm / 35").

Gauge

16 sts × 32 rows/rnds = 10 cm / 4" in Garter stitch flat on 5 mm / US 8 needles, after blocking.

18 sts × 30 rows/rnds = 10 cm / 4" in 1 × 1 rib flat on 3 mm / US 2.5 needles, after blocking.

Tip! When counting garter stitch row gauge each 'bump ridge' counts as two rows.

Needles

3 mm / US 2.5: circular needles 80–100 cm / 32–40" for rib hem, and DPNs for sleeve rib cuffs and front edge placket (or use the Magic Loop technique).

5 mm / US 8: circular needles 80–100 cm / 32–40" for body, and circular needles 40 cm / 16" for sleeves or DPNs (or use the Magic Loop technique).

Notions

Removable stitch markers, tapestry needle, stitch holder or scrap yarn, 4 buttons (diameter 22 mm / 0.75").

Suggested yarn

The cardigan is worked with one strand of DK / worsted weight yarn together with one strand of lace weight yarn.

You need approx.: **MC:** 755 (810, 865, 920) (970, 1025, 1080) (1135, 1190) m / 826 (887, 948, 1009) (1062, 1123, 1184) (1245, 1306) yds of DK or worsted weight yarn **together with** 755 (810, 865, 920) (970, 1025, 1080) (1135, 1190) m / 826 (887, 948, 1009) (1062, 1123, 1184) (1245, 1306) yds of lace weight yarn.

CC: 325 (380, 430, 485) (540, 595, 650) (700, 755) m / 355 (415, 470, 530) (590, 649, 710) (766, 826) yds of DK or worsted weight yarn **together with** 325 (380, 430, 485) (540, 595, 650) (700, 755) m / 355 (415, 470, 530) (590, 649, 710) (766, 826) yds lace weight yarn.

Sample knitted with yarns

MC: 350 (375, 400, 425) (450, 475, 500) (525, 550) g Sandnes Garn Double Sunday (100% merino wool – 108 m / 118 yds / 50 g) in the colour 5581 Sailor in the Dark **together with** 90 (95, 100, 110) (115, 120, 125) (135, 140) g Isager Silk Mohair (75% mohair, 15% silk – 212 m / 222 yds / 25 g) in the colour 100.

CC: 150 (175, 200, 225) (250, 275, 300) (325, 350) g Sandnes Garn Double Sunday (100% merino wool – 108 m / 118 yds / 50 g) in the colour 1012 Whipped Cream **together with** 40 (45, 50, 60) (65, 75, 80) (85, 90) g Filcolana Tilia (70% kid mohair, 30% mulberry silk – 210 m / 220 yds / 25 g) in the colour 101.

DIRECTIONS

The cardigan is worked from the top down making it easy to customise the length to suit your preferences and body perfectly. First the back is worked back and forth while shaping the shoulders. Stitches are picked up for the front edges separately, then all stitches are worked flat through the body. Stitches are picked up for the sleeves and worked in the round and lastly stitches are picked up along the front edges for a double knitted placket.

Upper Back

Top Section

With MC, cast on 26 (30, 30, 30) (30, 34, 34) (34, 36) sts with the Backwards Loop Cast-On method (or your preferred cast-on method) on 5 mm / US 8 needles.

Work the set-up row and place removable stitch markers in the first and last st to mark where sts will be picked up for the shoulder seams later. Work as follows:

Set-up row (WS): K1 and place removable stitch marker in this first st, k to last st, k1 and place removable stitch marker in this st. **Note!** These stitch markers aren't carried along the work.

Start shaping the back and shoulders as follows:

Row 1 (RS): Kfb, k to last st, kfb. 2 sts increased.
Row 2 (WS): Kfb, k to last st, kfb. 2 sts increased.

You have 30 (34, 34, 34) (34, 38, 38) (38, 40) sts.

Repeat rows 1–2, 12 (14, 16, 18) (20, 21, 22) (23, 24) more times.

You have 78 (90, 98, 106) (114, 122, 126) (130, 136) sts in total.

Place 2 new removable stitch markers into the first and last st to mark where sts will be picked up later for the shoulder seams.

Continue working with MC in Garter stitch (k every row) until total work measured from the cast-on edge is 17 (19, 21, 23) (25, 26, 27) (28, 29) cm / 6.75 (7.5, 8.25, 9) (9.75, 10.25, 10.75) (11, 11.5)" in total.

Tip! You can attach a stitch marker at the beginning of the RS rows to keep track of which side is RS and WS.

End after a WS row so that the next row is a RS row.

Stripe 1

Change to CC and work 20 rows in Garter stitch, end with a WS row.

The Upper Back is now complete. Cut the yarn and place sts on hold while you work the front next (you can, for example, transfer the sts onto a stitch wire or some scrap yarn).

Right Front

Top Section

With MC, pick up and k26 (30, 34, 38) (42, 44, 46) (48, 50) sts from the right outer edge to the right-side stitch marker (when looking at the piece with the RS facing you and the cast-on edge facing up towards the top) with 5 mm / US 8 needles, you can remove this marker now. Work 3 rows in Garter Stitch.

Next, begin shaping the shoulder by working decreases as follows:

Row 1 (RS): K2, ssk, k to end. 1 st decreased.
Rows 2–4: K to end.

There are 25 (29, 33, 37) (41, 43, 45) (47, 49) sts in total.

Repeat rows 1–4, 4 more times.

There are 21 (25, 29, 33) (37, 39, 41) (43, 45) sts in total.

Start shaping the front neckline as follows:

Row 1 (RS): K to last 2 sts, M1R, k2. 1 st increased.
Rows 2–4: K to end.

There are 22 (26, 30, 34) (38, 40, 42) (44, 46) sts in total.

Repeat rows 1–4, 1 (2, 2, 4) (4, 5, 5) (6, 6) more times.

There are 23 (28, 32, 38) (42, 45, 47) (50, 52) sts in total.

Stripe 1
Change to CC and work rows 1–4 (neckline shaping), 5 more times.

There are 28 (33, 37, 43) (47, 50, 52) (55, 57) sts in total.

Cut the yarn and place the sts on hold while you work the Left Front (ending on a WS row so that the next will be a RS row).

Left Front

Top Section

With MC, pick up and k26 (30, 34, 38) (42, 44, 46) (48, 50) sts from the left-side stitch marker to the outer left edge (when looking at the piece with the RS facing you and the cast-on edge facing up towards the top) with 5 mm / US 8 needles, you can remove this marker now.

Work 3 rows in Garter st.

Next, begin shaping the shoulder by working decreases as follows:

Row 1 (RS): K to last 4 sts, k2tog, k2. 1 st decreased.
Rows 2–4: K to end.

There are 25 (29, 33, 37) (41, 43, 45) (47, 49) sts in total.

Repeat rows 1–4, 4 more times.

There are 21 (25, 29, 33) (37, 39, 41) (43, 45) sts in total.

Start shaping the front neckline as follows:
Row 1 (RS): K2, M1L, k to end. 1 st increased.
Rows 2–4: K to end.

There are 22 (26, 30, 34) (38, 40, 42) (44, 46) sts in total.

Repeat rows 1–4, 1 (2, 2, 4) (4, 5, 5) (6, 6) more times.

There are 23 (28, 32, 38) (42, 45, 47) (50, 52) sts in total.

Stripe 1
Change to CC and work rows 1–4 (neckline shaping), 5 more times.

There are 28 (33, 37, 43) (47, 50, 52) (55, 57) sts in total.

You can cut the yarn as we'll change to MC when we join everything on the same circular needle for the body.

Body

Stripe 2
Next, change to MC and join the Left and Right Front sts with the Upper Back sts to work the body flat. The neckline will continue to be shaped and additional sts will be cast on for the underarms on the first row. Work as follows in MC:

Row 1 (RS): K2, M1L, k all remaining Left Front sts, cast on 6 (8, 8, 10) (10, 12, 12) (14, 14) sts with the Backwards Loop Cast-On method for the underarm sts, k all Upper Back sts, cast on 6 (8, 8, 10) (10, 12, 12) (14, 14) sts, k all Right Front sts until last 2 sts, M1R, k2. 2 sts increased.

There are 148 (174, 190, 214) (230, 248, 256) (270, 280) sts in total.

Work 3 rows in Garter st.

Continue shaping the neckline as follows:

Row 1 (RS): K2, M1L, k to last 2 sts, M1R, k2. 2 sts increased.
Rows 2–4: K to end.

There are 150 (176, 192, 216) (232, 250, 258) (272, 282) sts in total.

Repeat rows 1–4, 3 more times.

There are 156 (182, 198, 222) (238, 256, 264) (278, 288) sts in total.

Stripe 3
Change to CC and repeat rows 1–4, 2 more times.

There are 160 (186, 202, 226) (242, 260, 268) (282, 292) sts in total.

Continue with CC and work 12 rows in Garter st.

Stripe 4
Change to MC and work 20 rows in Garter st.

Stripe 5
Change to CC and work 20 rows in Garter st.

Bottom Section
Change to MC and work in Garter st until the body measured from the underarm is 25 (26, 27, 27) (28, 28, 29) (30, 30) cm / 9.75 (10.25, 10.75, 10.75) (11, 11, 11.5) (11.75, 11.75)" in total (or 5 cm / 2" less than total desired length). End on a WS row.

Work one set-up row before working the hem rib as follows:
Set-up row (RS): K1, k2tog, k to end.

There are 159 (185, 201, 225) (241, 259, 267) (281, 291) sts in total.

Change to 3 mm / US 2.5 needles and work the rib hem as follows:
Row 1 (WS): P2, *p1, k1* repeat to the last 3 sts, p3.
Row 2 (RS): K2, *k1, p1* repeat to the last 3 sts, k3.
Row 3 (WS): P2, *p1, k1* repeat to the last 3 sts, p3.

Repeat rows 2–3 until the rib hem measures 5 cm / 2" in length. Bind off using the Italian Bind-Off method.

Sleeves

The sleeve sts are picked up and k along the armhole openings. The sleeves are worked in the rnd in Garter st on either 5 mm / US 8 (40–60 cm / 16–24") circular needles, double–pointed needles or a longer circular needle for the Magic Loop technique.

Work as follows:
With MC and the RS facing, pick up and k58 (62, 64, 68) (72, 74, 76) (78, 80) sts evenly around the armhole opening starting from the middle of the underarm. Join to work in the rnd and place a marker to mark the beginning of rnd.

Stripe 1
Work 20 rnds of Garter st in MC as follows:

Rnds 1, 3, 5, 7, 9, 11, 13, 15, 17, 19: K all sts.
Rnds 2, 4, 6, 8, 10, 12, 14, 16, 18, 20: P all sts.

Stripe 2
Change to CC and work 20 rnds of Garter st.

Stripe 3
Change to MC and work 20 rnds of Garter st.

Stripe 4
Change to CC and work 20 rnds of Garter st.

Stripe 5
Change to MC and work 20 rnds of Garter st.

Stripe 6
Change to CC and work 20 rnds of Garter st.

Bottom section
Change to MC and continue working in Garter st until the sleeve measures 42 cm / 16.5" (or 5 cm / 2" less than total desired length) from underarm.

Only sizes L (XL, 2XL, 3XL) (4XL, 5XL)
Work one rnd of decreases before beginning the cuff as follows:

Size L: *K15, k2tog* 4 times. 4 sts decreased.
Size XL: *K7, k2tog* 8 times. 8 sts decreased.
Size 2XL: K2, *k7, k2tog* 8 times.
8 sts decreased.
Size 3XL: K4, *k7, k2tog* 8 times.
8 sts decreased.
Size 4XL: *K11, k2tog* 6 times.
6 sts decreased.
Size 5XL: *K6, k2tog* 10 times.
8 sts decreased.

There are 58 (62, 64, 64) (64, 66, 68) (72, 72) sts in total.

Change to 3 mm / US 2.5 needles and work *k1, p1* ribbing until the cuff measures 5 cm / 2" in total.

Bind off using the Italian Bind-Off method.

Work the other sleeve the same.

Front Edge Placket

For the front edge placket, sts are picked up along the front edges and back neck cast-on edge with a 3 mm / US 2.5 circular needle. The front placket is worked in double knitting with a 3 mm / US 2.5 double-pointed needle.

4 buttonholes are worked on the left side Front Edge Placket.

Start by picking up and knitting sts as follows: Pick up and k 1 st in every st along the front edges and back neck cast on edge with a 3 mm / US 2.5 80–100 cm or a longer needle (or, you can also use two circular needles for this). The amount of picked up sts will depend a bit on how long your cardigan is. Cut the yarn.

Place 4 removable stitch markers to mark where the bottom of the buttonholes will be worked along the left front edge of the cardigan (when looking at the cardigan in front of you with RS facing up). Place the bottom buttonhole 4 sts from the bottom edge of the hem and place the top buttonhole just below the last increase done for the neckline. Place the 2 remaining buttonholes at an equal distance apart between the top and bottom buttonhole.

See the instructions on how to work the buttonholes below.

Join in new yarn and start working the double knitted placket from the bottom left front edge (when looking at the cardigan with the front and RS facing you).

Work as follows:
Cast on 11 new sts on the 3 mm / US 2.5 circular needle in addition to the picked up sts on the left front edge of the cardigan using the Italian Cast-On method (make the first and last st of the cast on sts purl sts).

Row 1 (RS): *K1, sl1 wyif* repeat a total of 5 times, k2tog tbl (k the last st of the 11 that you just cast on together with one st from the picked up sts through the back loops). Turn work.
Row 2 (WS): *Sl1 wyif, k1* repeat to the last st, sl1 wyif. Turn work.

Repeat rows 1–2 across all the picked up sts along the front edges and back neck until there is only 1 of the picked-up sts left (until there are only 12 sts remaining on the needle) **while at the same time** working 4 buttonholes along the left front edge at your markers.

Bind off from the RS using the Italian Bind-Off method. When working the last 2 sts of the Italian Bind-Off, seam these 2 sts as if they were 1 st (as if you had knitted them together tbl).

Buttonholes

To create the buttonholes the front edge placket is divided into two parts and each side of the buttonhole is knitted separately one at a time. After working each buttonhole, the two parts or 'columns' are joined together again. Start working the buttonholes where the markers are placed.

First work one side of the buttonholes across the first 6 sts. Work from the RS as follows:
Row 1 (RS): *K1, sl1 wyif* repeat a total of 3 times. Turn work.
Row 2 (WS): *K1, sl1 wyif* work a total of 3 times. Turn work.

Repeat rows 1–2, 3 more times (work 8 rows in total).

Repeat row 1 (RS) once more, so that the working yarn is now in the middle of the front edge placket sts. Cut the yarn and let the sts rest on a stitch holder or an extra double-pointed needle while working the other side of the buttonhole.

Join new yarn and work from the RS as follows:
Row 1 (RS): *K1, sl1 wyif* repeat a total of 2 times, k2tog tbl. Turn work.
Row 2 (WS): *Sl1 wyif, k1* repeat to the last st, sl1 wyif. Turn work.

Repeat rows 1–2, 3 more times (work 8 rows in total).

Repeat row 1 (RS) once more, so the next row is a WS row.

Now join both sides of the button-hole together on the same needle, work as follows:

Row 1 (WS): *Sl1 wyif, k1* repeat across all the front edge placket sts to the last st, sl1 wyif. Turn work.

The buttonhole is now complete. The next row is a RS row.

Finishing

Weave in all ends.

Tip! You can carefully weave in the yarn ends at the top and bottom of the buttonholes into the seam between the front edge placket sts and pick up edge.

Spread out the buttons along the right front edge (when looking at the cardigan in front of you with the RS facing up) so that they correspond with the button-holes on the left side. Attach them by hand sewing.

STYLING TIP #10

Add a touch of whimsy to your look by layering your chunky knit over a top with delicate lace peeking out at the neckline. It's the perfect way to balance cosy and chic, giving your outfit a soft, feminine twist that's both unexpected and effortlessly charming.

This simple and stylish hat is worked from the bottom up. The design, together with the wide folded brim, gives the Chloe beanie a contemporary, laid-back look that makes it easy to wear with any outfit. It's also an excellent project when you want something easy and fuss-free on your needles, as the Stockinette stitch makes it quick and relaxing to knit up.

CHLOE

Sizes

One size.

Finished garment measurements

Circumference: 46 cm / 18.5".
Total length: 29 cm / 11.5".
Total length with folded rib brim:
21 cm / 8.25".

The beanie has quite a bit of negative ease because it stretches a lot and will fit over most adult size heads.

Gauge

20 sts × 30 rnds = 10 cm / 4" on 4 mm / US 6 needles in Stockinette st, after blocking.

26 sts × 30 rnds = 10 cm / 4" on 3 mm / US 2.5 needles in 1 × 1 rib, after blocking.

Needles

3 mm / US 2.5: circular needles 40–60 cm / 16–24" (or longer ones for the Magic Loop technique) for rib.

4 mm / US 6: circular needles 40–60 cm / 16–24" (or longer ones for the Magic Loop technique) and DPNs (if you're not using the Magic Loop technique) for Stockinette st and crown shaping.

Notions

Stitch markers, tapestry needle.

Suggested yarn

The beanie is worked by holding two strands of lace weight yarn together with one strand of fingering weight yarn.

You need approx. 225 m / 246 yds of fingering weight yarn and 500 m / 547 yds m of lace weight yarn.

Sample knitted with yarns

50 g Knitting for Olive Soft Silk Mohair (70% mohair, 30% silk – 225 m / 246 yds / 25 g) in the colour Brown Nougat **together with** 50 g Knitting for Olive Merino (100% merino wool – 250 m / 273 yds / 50 g) in the colour Brown Nougat.

The beanie is worked holding two strands of silk-mohair and one strand of merino together.

DIRECTIONS

The hat is worked bottom up in the round. The folded brim is worked in a 1 x 1 rib and the beanie is worked in Stockinette stitch. The crown is shaped by working decreases.

Brim

Cast on 92 sts with 3 mm / US 2.5 circular needles with the Long Tail Cast-On method. Join in the rnd and place a marker to indicate the beginning of the rnd (= BOR-m).

Work 22 rnds of *k1, p1* ribbing, or until the work measures 7.5 cm / 3" in total. Then, work one rnd of k sts across all sts, this will help the edge of the brim to fold up nicely.

Continue working 20 rnds of *k1, p1* ribbing, or until work measures 14 cm / 5.5" in total.

Beanie

Change to 4 mm / US 6 circular needles and continue working in Stockinette st until the beanie measures 6.5 cm / 2.5" from ribbing (or 20.5 cm / 8" in total).

Shaping the crown

Next, you might want to transfer all sts to 4 mm / US 6 DPNs (if you're not using the Magic Loop technique) when shaping the crown.

Rnd 1: K46, PM, k to end of rnd.
Rnd 2: K1, ssk, k to 3 sts before marker, k2tog, k1, SM, k1, ssk, k to 3 sts before marker, k2tog, k1. 4 sts decreased.

There are 88 sts in total.

Rnd 3: K all sts.

Repeat rnds 2–3, 4 more times.

16 sts decreased, there are 72 sts in total.

Then repeat rnd 2, 14 more times.

56 sts decreased, there are 16 sts in total.

Next rnd: *K2tog* to end of rnd.

You have 8 sts in total.

Cut the yarns and pull through the remaining sts.

Finishing

Weave in all ends and fold up the brim at the purl edge.

This simple and stylish top features narrow shoulders for a flattering silhouette and a wide rib collar that adds a chic, slightly dressy touch. Worked from the bottom up, Sundazed is a fun and quick knit, with the Stockinette stitch making it a relaxing project. Choose a cotton or silk yarn for a breezy fabric that's perfect for warm days, or warmer wool or even silk mohair for a top that can be styled underneath a blazer for chillier weather.

SUNDAZED

STYLING TIP #11
Elevate a simple summer top by pairing it with straight-leg pants in a matching shade for a cohesive city look. The tonal harmony creates a streamlined silhouette, making your outfit look polished yet laid-back, perfect for those warm, sunny days.

Sizes

XS (S, M, L) (XL, 2XL, 3XL) (4XL, 5XL)

Finished garment measurements

Bust circumference: 80 (87.5, 95, 100) (110, 120, 130) (140, 150) cm / 31.5 (34.5, 37.5, 39.5) (43.25, 47.25, 51.25) (55, 59)".

Length from underarm to hem: 27 (27, 27, 27) (29, 30, 30) (32, 32) cm / 10.75 (10.75, 10.75, 10.75) (11.5, 11.75, 11.75) (12.5, 12.5)" (or desired length).

The Sundazed top is designed to have 5–10 cm / 2–4" of negative ease for a regular fit (the fabric will stretch out when worn).

Sample shown in size S (Kika has a bust of approx. 89 cm / 35").

Gauge

16 sts × 24 rows/rnds = 10 cm / 4" in Stockinette st on 4 mm / US 6 needles, after blocking.

17 sts × 28 rows/rnds = 10 cm / 4" in 1 × 1 rib on 3 mm / US2.5 needles, after blocking.

Needles

3 mm / US 2.5: circular needles 40–60 cm / 16–24" for collar and hem rib.

4 mm / US 6: circular needles 60–100 cm / 24–40" for body.

Notions

Stitch markers, tapestry needle, stitch holder or scrap yarn.

Suggested yarn

The top can be worked with one strand of DK weight yarn or by holding two strands of sport / fingering weight yarn together.

You need approx. 720 (810, 900, 990) (1080, 1170, 1260) (1350, 1440) m / 787 (886, 984, 1083) (1181, 1280, 1378) (1476, 1575) yds of fingering or sport weight yarn or 360 (405, 450, 495) (540, 585, 630) (675, 720) m / 394 (443, 492, 542) (591, 640, 689) (738, 787) yds of DK weight yarn.

Sample knitted with yarns

200 (225, 250, 275) (300, 325, 375) (400, 425) g of Sandnes Garn Mandarin Petit (100% cotton – 180 m / 197 yds per 50 g) in the colour Sand 2724.

The top is worked by holding two strands together.

DIRECTIONS

The Sundazed top is worked from bottom up. First the body is worked in the round up until the armholes. Then the work is separted and the upper front and back are worked separately flat and the shoulder seams are grafted together. Lastly stitches are picked up from the neckline for the ribbed collar which is worked to double length and folded and attached on the inside.

Body

The Body is worked in the rnd from bottom up.

Cast on 128 (140, 152, 160) (176, 192, 208) (224, 240) sts for 1 × 1 rib using the Long Tail Cast-On method with 3 mm / US 2.5 (60–100 cm / 24–40") circular needles.

Join to work in the rnd and place a stitch marker to indicate beginning of rnd (= BOR–m).

Work *k1, p1* rib until the hem measures 4 cm / 1.5".

Change to 4 mm / US 6 (60–100 cm / 24–40") circular needles and work in Stockinette st until the body measures 27 (27, 27, 27) (29, 30, 30) (32, 32) cm / 10.75 (10.75, 10.75, 10.75) (11.5, 11.75, 11.75) (12.5, 12.5)" in total from the cast-on edge.

Upper Back

The sts for the Upper Front are put on hold while working the Upper Back flat.

Work as follows:
Row 1 (RS): K64 (70, 76, 80) (88, 96, 104) (112, 120) sts, transfer the remaining 64 (70, 76, 80) (88, 96, 104) (112, 120) sts onto a stitch holder or scrap yarn while working the Upper Back.
Row 2 (WS): P64 (70, 76, 80) (88, 96, 104) (112, 120).
Row 3: K2, ssk, k to last 4 sts, k2tog, k2. 2 sts decreased.
Row 4: P to end.

There are 62 (68, 74, 78) (86, 94, 102) (110, 118) sts in total.

Repeat rows 3–4, 11 (12, 13, 13) (15, 17, 18) (21, 22) more times.

There are 40 (44, 48, 52) (56, 60, 66) (68, 74) sts in total.

Work 10 (10, 12, 14) (14, 14, 16) (18, 18) more rows in Stockinette st, ending on a WS row (so that the next row is a RS row).

Left Back Shoulder

The Left and Right Back shoulders are worked separately while shaping the back neckline.

Begin by binding off sts for the middle of the back neckline. Work as follows:

Row 1 (RS): K14 (15, 15, 16) (17, 19, 21) (22, 24) sts, bind off the next 12 (14, 18, 20) (22, 22, 24) (24, 26) sts, k 14 (15, 15, 16) (17, 19, 21) (22, 24) remaining sts.

Shape the left side of the back neckline as follows:

Row 2 (WS): P14 (15, 15, 16) (17, 19, 21) (22, 24).
Row 3: K2, ssk, k to end. 1 st decreased.
Row 4: P to end.

Repeat rows 3–4, 3 (3, 3, 3) (3, 4, 4) (5, 5) more times.

There are 10 (11, 11, 12) (13, 14, 16) (16, 18) sts in total.

Work 10 (10, 12, 14) (14, 14, 16) (18, 18) more rows in Stockinette st, ending on a WS row (so that the next row is a RS row).

Cut the yarn and transfer the sts onto a stitch wire or scrap yarn (the sts will be grafted together with the front shoulder sts in the end so that the seam becomes invisible).

Right Back Shoulder

Facing the WS, join in new yarn and begin working the right shoulder. **Note!** the first row is a WS row.

Shape the right side of the back neckline as follows:

Row 1 (WS): P14 (15, 15, 16) (17, 19, 21) (22, 24) sts.
Row 2 (RS): K to last 4 sts, k2tog, k2tog, k2. 1 st decreased.
Row 3: P to end.

Repeat rows 3–4, 3 (3, 3, 3) (3, 4, 4) (5, 5) more times.

There are 10 (11, 11, 12) (13, 14, 16) (16, 18) sts in total.

Work 10 (10, 12, 14) (14, 14, 16) (18, 18) more rows in Stockinette st, ending on a WS row (so that the next row is a RS row). Cut the yarn and transfer the sts onto a stitch wire or scrap yarn (the sts will be grafted together with the front shoulder sts in the end so that the seam becomes invisible).

Upper Front

The Upper Front is worked flat. Facing the WS, begin by transferring the 64 (70, 76, 80) (88, 96, 104) (112, 120) front sts that you had on hold onto 4 mm / US 6 circular needles.

Work as follows:
Row 1 (RS): K 64 (70, 76, 80) (88, 96, 104) (112, 120).
Row 2 (WS): P to end.
Row 3 (RS): K2, ssk, k to last 4 sts, k2tog, k2. 2 sts decreased.
Row 4: P to end.

There are 62 (68, 74, 78) (86, 94, 102) (110, 118) sts in total.

Repeat rows 3–4, 11 (12, 13, 13) (15, 17, 18) (21, 22) more times.

There are 40 (44, 48, 52) (56, 60, 66) (68, 74) sts in total.

Work 4 (4, 6, 6) (6, 6, 8) (10, 10) more rows in Stockinette st, ending on a WS row (so that the next row is a RS row).

Left Front Shoulder

Next the Left and Right fronts are worked separately while shaping the neckline.

Begin by binding off sts for the middle of the front neckline, work as follows:

Row 1 (RS): K14 (15, 15, 16) (17, 19, 21) (22, 24) sts, bind off the next 12 (14, 18, 20) (22, 22, 24) (24, 26) sts, k 14 (15, 15, 16) (17, 19, 21) (22, 24) remaining sts.

Shape the left side of the neckline as follows:

Row 2 (WS): P14 (15, 15, 16) (17, 19, 21) (22, 24).
Row 3: K2, ssk, k to end. 1 st decreased.
Row 4: P to end.

Repeat rows 3–4, 3 (3, 3, 3) (3, 4, 4) (5, 5) more times.

There are 10 (11, 11, 12) (13, 14, 16) (16, 18) sts in total.

Work 16 (16, 18, 22) (22, 22, 24) (26, 26) more rows in Stockinette st, ending on a WS row.

Cut the yarn and transfer the sts onto a stitch wire or scrap yarn.

Right Front Shoulder

Facing the WS, join in new yarn and begin working the right shoulder.

Shape the right side of the neckline as follows:

Row 1 (WS): P14 (15, 15, 16) (17, 19, 21) (22, 24).
Row 2 (RS): K to last 4 sts, k2tog, k2tog, k2. 1 st decreased.
Row 3: P to end.

Repeat rows 3–4, 3 (3, 3, 3) (3, 4, 4) (5, 5) more times.

There are 10 (11, 11, 12) (13, 14, 16) (16, 18) sts in total.

Work 16 (16, 18, 22) (22, 22, 24) (26, 26) rows in Stockinette st, ending on a WS row.

Cut the yarn and transfer the sts into a stitch holder or scrap yarn.

Shoulder seams

Graft the back and front shoulders together so that the join becomes invisible.

Collar

With 3 mm / US 2.5 (40–60 cm / 16–24") circular needles, starting at one of the shoulder seams, pick up and k92 (92, 94, 98) (98, 98, 100) (102, 102) sts evenly from around the neckline opening. Join to work in the rnd and place BOR-m.

Work *k1, p1* rib until the collar measures 7.5 cm / 3" and bind off using the Standard Bind-Off method loosely.

Finishing

Weave in all ends. Fold the collar double and attach it on the inside by sewing.

Named for the repeating lace stitches that look like hearts, Sweetheart features a soft, delicate design that never goes out of style. The decorative lace creates a light and airy feel, making it the perfect sweater for those looking for a project with a fabric that isn't too thick or heavy yet still keeps you warm.

SWEET-HEART

26
22
36
37
29
47
3
42

Sizes

XS (S, M, L) (XL, 2XL, 3XL) (4XL, 5XL)

Finished garment measurements

Bust circumference: 79 (86.5, 94, 105) (115, 125, 130) (133, 138) cm / 31 (34, 37, 41.25) (45.25, 49.25, 51) (52.25, 54.25)".

Length from underarm to hem: 23.5 (28, 28, 29.5) (32, 32, 32.5) (36, 36) cm / 9.25 (11, 11, 11.5) (12.5, 12.5, 12.75) (14, 14)".

Sleeve length from underarm: 45 (47.5, 47.5, 47.5) (47.5, 47.5, 51) (51, 51) cm / 17.75 (18.75, 18.75, 18.75) (18.75, 18.75, 20) (20, 20)".

Upper sleeve circumference: 36.5 (39, 41.5, 49.5) (53, 57, 60.5) (64.5, 72) cm / 14.5 (15.25, 16.25, 19.5) (20.75, 22.5, 23.75) (25.5, 28.25)".

The Sweetheart sweater is designed to have 0–10 cm / 0–4" positive ease.

Note! The sweater will most likely stretch out a bit when worn since the lace stitch fabric is soft and stretchy.

Sample shown is size S (Kika has a bust of approx. 89 cm / 35").

Gauge

16 sts × 26 rnds = 10 cm / 4" on 4.5 mm / US 7 needles in Chart B, after blocking.

Needles

3 mm / US 2.5: circular needles 40–60 cm / 16–24" for neck opening and 80–100 cm / 32–40" for hem rib, and DPNs for sleeve rib (or use the Magic Loop technique instead).

4.5 mm / US 7: circular needles 40–60 cm / 16–24" for the sleeves and 80–100 cm / 32–40" for body, or just 80–100 cm / 32–40" needles if you're using the Magic Loop technique.

Notions

Cable needle or DPN, removable (open) stitch markers, tapestry needle, stitch holders or scrap yarn.

Suggested yarn

The sweater is worked with two strands of lace weight yarn and one strand of fingering weight yarn.

You need approx. 1750 (1875, 2000, 2125) (2250, 2375, 2500) (2750, 2875) m / 1914 (2050, 2187, 2324) (2460, 2597, 2734) (3008, 3144) yds of fingering weight yarn **together with** 3500 (3750, 4000, 4250) (4500, 4750, 5000) (5500, 5750) m / 3828 (4101, 4374, 4648) (4921, 5195, 5468) (6015, 6288) yds of lace weight yarn.

Sample knitted with yarns

375 (400, 425, 450) (475, 500, 525) (550, 575) g Knitting for Olive Merino (100% merino wool – 250 m / 273 yds / 50 g) in the colour Rose Clay **together with** 100 (110, 115, 120) (125, 135, 140) (155, 160) g Knitting for Olive Soft Silk Mohair (70% mohair, 30% silk – 225 m / 246 yds / 25 g) in the colour Rose Clay **together with** 100 (110, 115, 120) (125, 135, 140) (155, 160) g Knitting for Olive Soft Silk Mohair in the colour Dusty Rose.

The sweater is worked by holding two strands of silk mohair and one strand of merino together.

DIRECTIONS

The sweater is worked top down seamlessly. Firstly the collar is worked in a twisted rib stitch to double length, it will be folded and attached on the inside at the end. The increases for the yoke are incorporated into the lace stitch pattern which is both fun and engaging to knit. The sleeves are worked in the round and finished with a twisted rib cuff for a slight balloon-shape.

Collar

Cast on 100 (100, 100, 108) (108, 108, 116) (116, 116) sts with 3 mm / US 2.5 circular needles (40–60 cm / 16–24") using the Backwards Loop Cast-On method.
Note! The cast on edge will be hidden when the collar is folded inside and sewn.

Join to work in the rnd and place a marker to indicate the beginning of rnd (=BOR-marker).

Work *k1 tbl, p1* rib until work measures 7.5 cm / 3" in total.

Yoke

Change to 4.5 mm / US 7 circular needles (80–100 cm / 32–40") and work one set-up rnd as follows:

Set-up rnd:
Sizes XS, S and M: K all sts.
Sizes L, XL, 2XL: *K6, M1R* across all sts.
Sizes 3XL, 4XL and 5XL: K2, *k1, M1R, k2, M1R* across all sts.

There are 100 (100, 100, 126) (126, 126, 192) (192, 192) sts in total.

Start working according to Chart A in your chosen size [chart repeats 10 (10, 10, 14) (14, 14, 16) (16, 16) times across yoke sts] until all rnds 1–45 (1–47, 1–54, 1–54) (1–57, 1–64, 1–66) (1–69, 1–69) are complete.

There are 210 (230, 250, 294) (322, 350, 384) (416, 448) sts in total.

Body

Work the body and put the sts for the sleeves on hold. Work as follows:

Rnd 1: Work rnd 1 of Chart B, *work rnd 1 of Chart C, work rnd 1 of Chart B* 2 (2, 2, 3) (3, 3, 4) (4, 4) times (= back), transfer 50 (54, 58, 71) (77, 83, 83) (89, 95) sleeve sts onto a holder (for example a stitch wire or just a long piece of yarn), cast on 8 (8, 8, 8) (8, 8, 11) (11, 11) sts for underarm with the Backwards Loop Cast-On method, work rnd 1 of Chart B, *work rnd 1 of Chart C, work rnd 1 of Chart B* 2 (2, 2, 3) (3, 3, 4) (4, 4) times (= front), transfer 50 (54, 58, 71) (77, 83, 83) (89, 95) sleeve sts onto a holder, cast on 8 (8, 8, 8) (8, 8, 11) (11, 11) sts for underarm with the Backwards Loop Cast-On method. Place a marker to indicate the beginning of rnd (= BOR-m).

There are 126 (138, 150, 168) (184, 200, 240) (260, 280) sts for the body.

Rnd 2: *Work rnd 2 of Chart B, work rnd 2 of Chart C* across all sts.
Rnd 3: *Work the next rnd of Chart B, work the next rnd of Chart C* across all sts.

Continue working as established until all rnds 1–8 (1–10, 1–10, 1–8) (1–10, 1–10, 1–10) (1–10, 1–10) of Charts B and C are completed a total of 6 (6, 6, 8) (7, 7, 9) (8, 8) times or until work measures approx. 18.5 (23, 23, 24.5) (27, 27, 27.5) (31, 31) cm (or until work measures approx. 5 cm / 2" less than desired total length).

Change to 3 mm / US 2.5 circular needles and work *k1 tbl, p1* rib until the hem measures 5 cm / 2" and bind off using the Standard Bind-Off method (or your preferred bind-off method).

Sleeves

Transfer 50 (54, 58, 71) (77, 83, 83) (89, 95) sleeve sts that you had on hold onto 4.5 mm / US 7 (40–60 cm / 16–24") circular needles, DPNs or longer needles if you're using the Magic Loop technique.

Rnd 1: Starting from the middle of underarm, pick up and k 4 (4, 4, 4) (4, 4, 6) (6, 6) sts, PM, work rnd 1 of Chart C, *work rnd 1 of Chart B, work rnd 1 of Chart C* 2 (2, 2, 3) (3, 3, 3) (3, 3) times, PM, pick up and k 4 (4, 4, 4) (4, 4, 5) (5, 5) sts from underarm. Place a marker to indicate the beginning of rnd (= BOR-m).

There are 58 (62, 66, 79) (85, 91, 94) (100, 106) sts in total for the sleeve.

Rnd 2: K to m, SM, work rnd 2 of Chart C, *work rnd 2 of Chart B, work rnd 2 of Chart C* to m, SM, k to end.

Rnds 3–8 (3–10, 3–10, 3–8) (3–10, 3–10, 3–10) (3–10, 3–10): K to m, SM, work the next rnd of Chart C, *work the next rnd of Chart B, work the next rnd of Chart C* to m, SM, k to end.

Rnd 9 (11, 11, 9) (11, 11, 11) (11, 11): K2tog, k to m, SM, work rnd 1 of Chart C, *work rnd 1 of Chart B, work rnd 1 of Chart C* to m, SM, k to last 2 sts, ssk. 2 sts decreased.

There are 56 (60, 64, 77) (83, 89, 92) (98, 104) sts in total for the sleeve.

Rnds 10–16 (12–20, 12–20, 10–16) (12–20, 12–20, 10–20) (12–20, 12–20): K to m, SM, work the next rnd of Chart C, *work the next rnd of Chart B, work the next rnd of Chart C* to m, SM, k to end.

Rnds 17–32 (21–40, 21–40, 17–32) (21–40, 21–40, 21–40) (21–40, 21–40): Continue working like this repeating rnds 9–16 (11–20, 11–20, 9–16) (11–20,11–20, 11–20) (11–20, 11–20), 2 (2, 2, 2) (2, 2, 3) (3, 3) more times [meaning you'll have completed all rnds of the charts a total of 4 (4, 4, 4) (4, 4, 5) (5, 5) times for the sleeve].

There are 52 (56, 60, 73) (79, 85, 86) (92, 98) sts in total.

Rnd 33 (41, 41, 33) (41, 41, 41) (41, 41): K to m, SM, work rnd 1 of Chart C, *work rnd 1 of Chart B, work rnd 1 of Chart C* to m, SM, k to end.

Rnds 34–104 (42–110, 42–110, 34–112) (42–110, 42–110, 41–110) (42–110, 42–110): Continue working as established always working the next rnd of Chart B and C until all rnds are completed 9 (7, 7, 10) (7, 7, 10) (7, 7) more times, or until the sleeve measures approx. 40 (43, 43, 43) (43, 43, 46) (46, 46) cm / 15.75 (17, 17, 17) (17, 17, 18) (18, 18)" from underarm [meaning you'll have completed all rnds of the charts a total of 13 (11, 11, 14) (11, 11, 15) (12, 12) times for the sleeve].

Change to 3 mm / US 2.5 circular needles and work as follows:

Size XS
K1, p1, *k1, p1, k2tog, p1, k1, p2tog* to last 2 sts, k1, p1. 12 sts decreased.

Size S
K1, p1, k1, p1, *k1, p1, k2tog, p1, k1, p2tog* to last 4 sts, k1, p1, k1, p1. 12 sts decreased.

Size M
K1, p1, k1, p1, k2tog, p1, k1, p1, k1, p2tog to end of rnd. 10 sts decreased.

Size L
K2tog, p1, *k1, p1, k1, p1, k1, p2tog* to end of rnd. 11 sts decreased.

Size XL
K2tog, p1, k2tog, p1, k2tog, p1, *k1, p1, k1, p1, k1, p2tog* to end of rnd. 13 sts decreased.

Size 2XL
K1, p1, k1, p2tog to end of rnd. 17 sts decreased.

Size 3XL
K1, p1, *k1, p1, k1, p2tog* to end of rnd. 18 sts decreased.

Size 4XL
K1, p1, k1, p1, *k2tog, p1, k1, p1, k1, p2tog* to end of rnd. 22 sts decreased.

Size 5XL
K1, p1, *k1, p1, k2tog, p1, k1, p2tog* to end of rnd. 24 sts decreased.

There are 40 (44, 50, 62) (66, 68, 68) (70, 74) sts in total.

Work *k1 tbl, p1* rib until the cuff measures 5 cm / 2" and bind off using Standard Bind-Off method (or your preferred bind-off method).

Work the other sleeve the same.

Finishing

Fold the collar double and attach it by hand sewing loosely on the inside to prevent the neckline from becoming too tight. Weave in all loose ends.

CHART A

XS

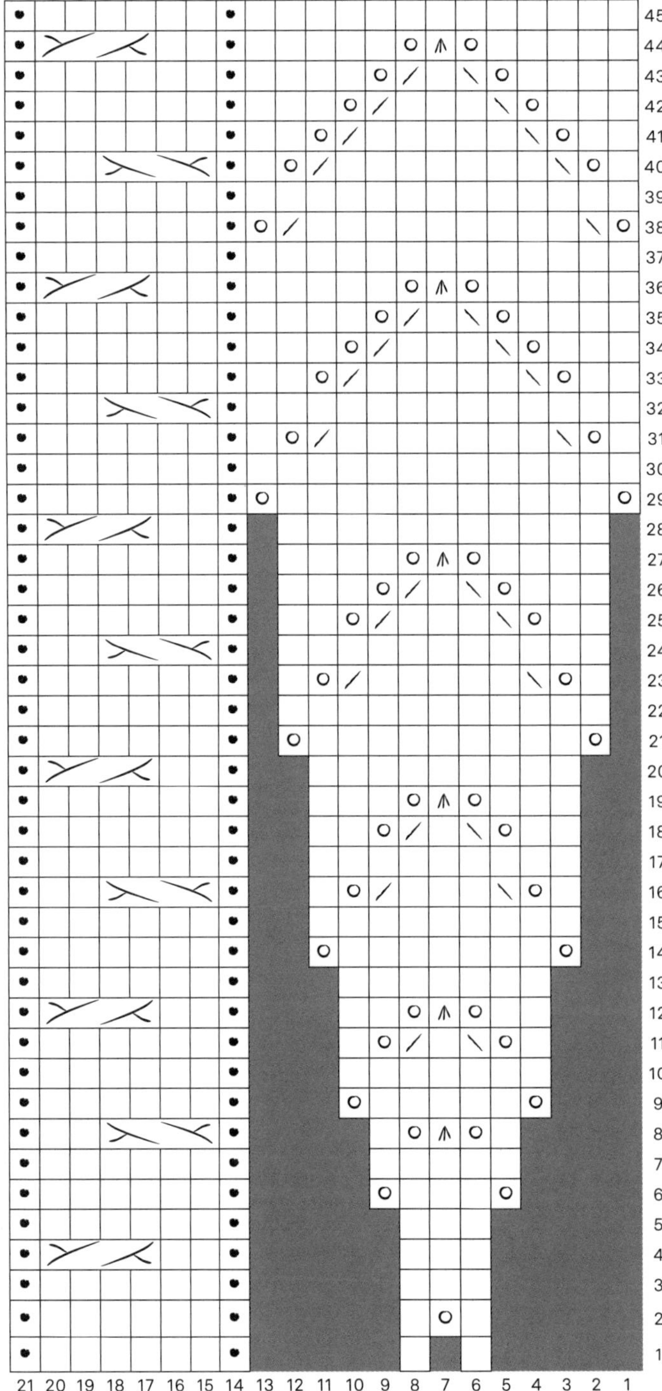

CHART A

S

knit
purl
yo
knit 2 together
ssk
2/2 LC
2/2 RC
slip 1, knit 2 together, pull slipped stitch over k2tog
no stitch

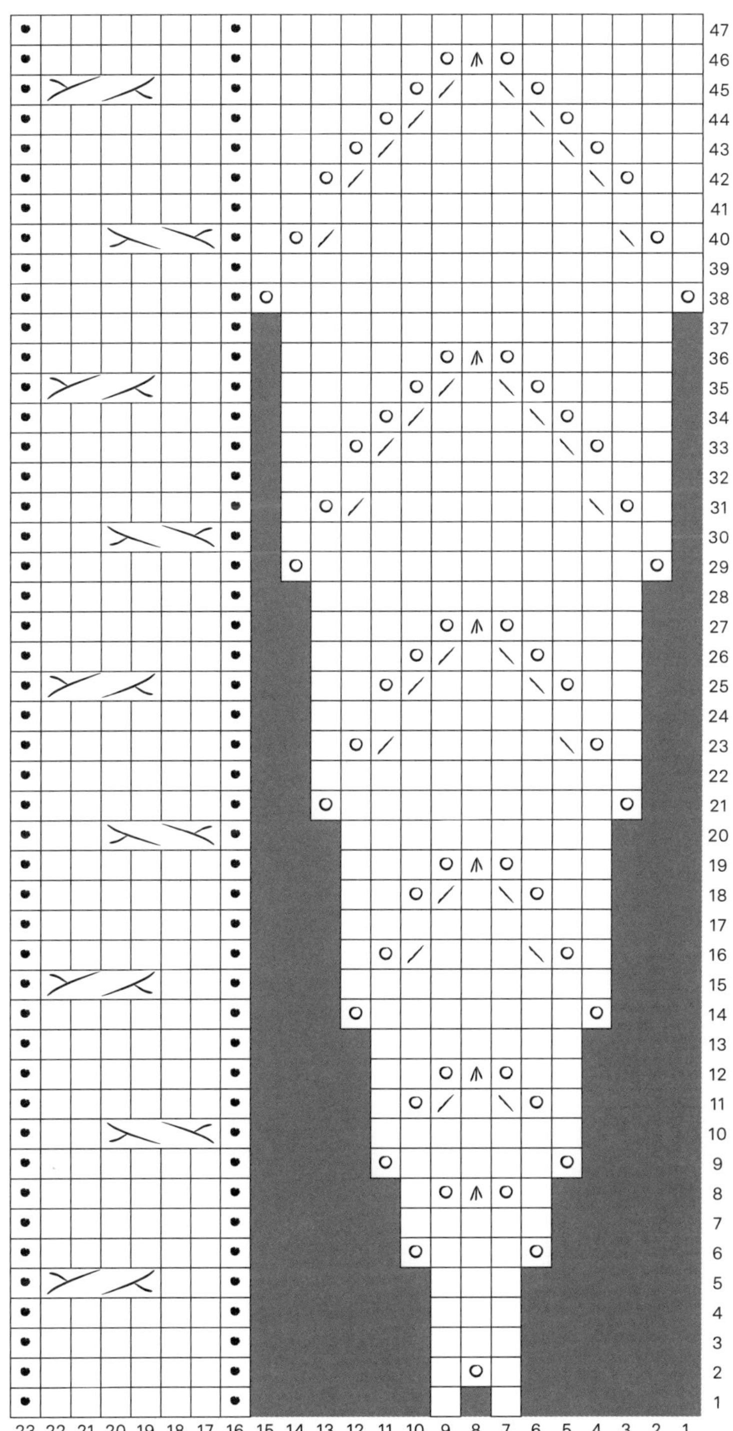

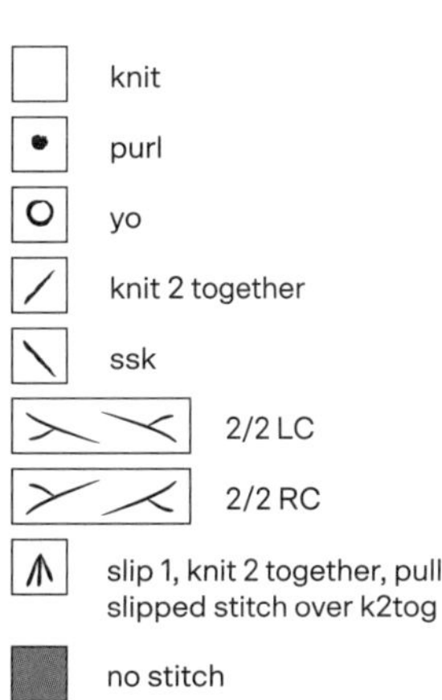

CHART A

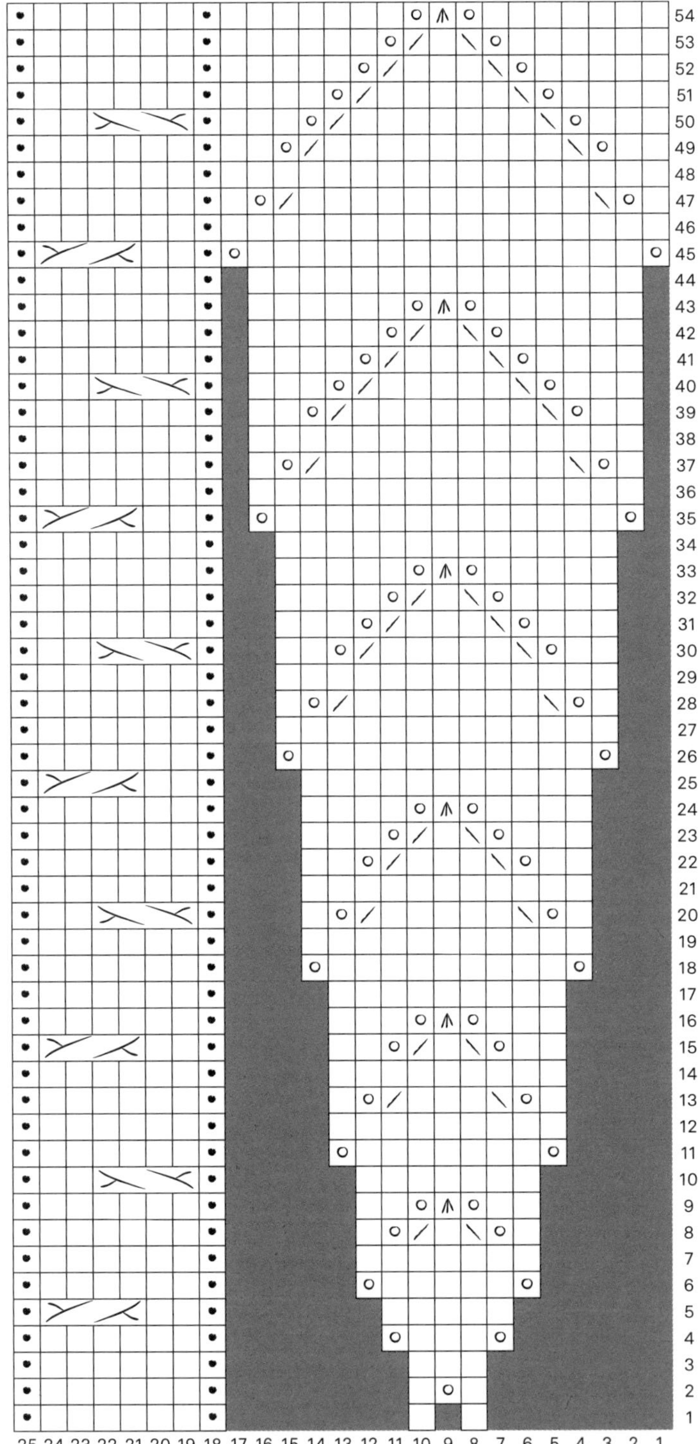

CHART A

L

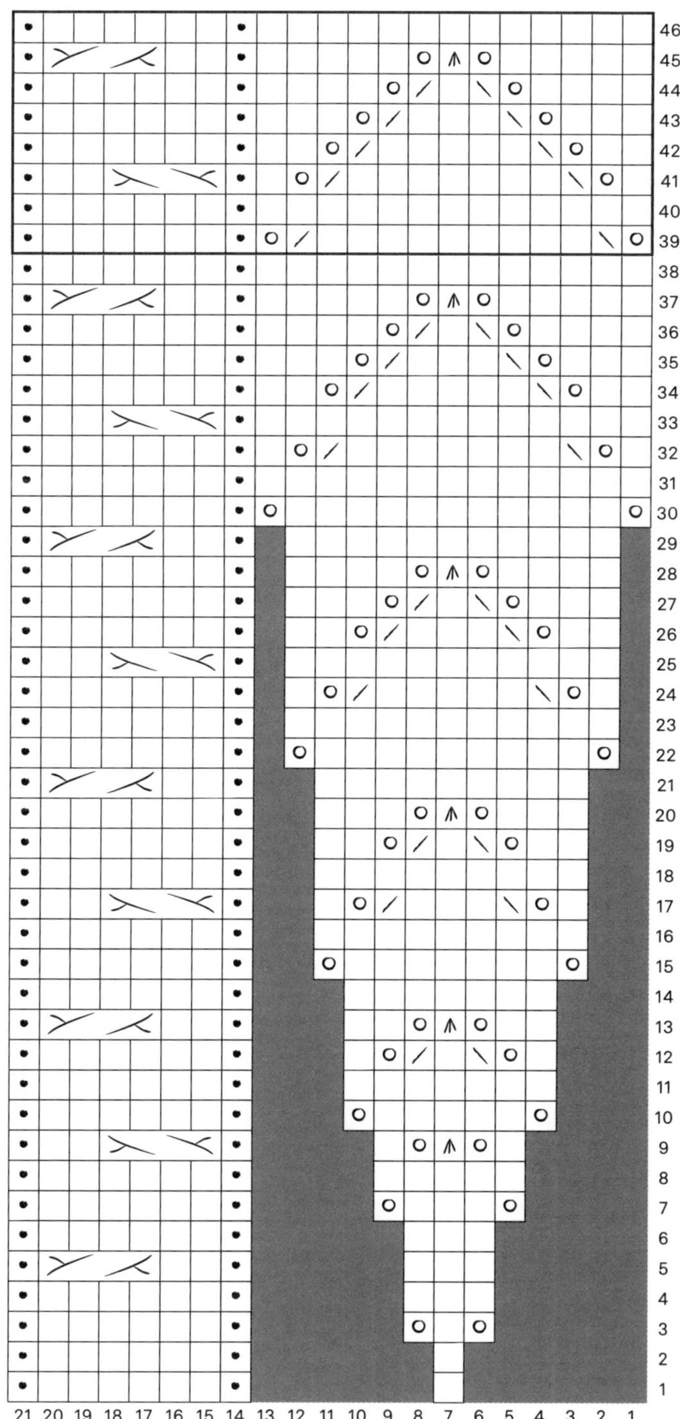

- knit
- purl
- yo
- knit 2 together
- ssk
- 2/2 LC
- 2/2 RC
- slip 1, knit 2 together, pull slipped stitch over k2tog
- no stitch
- repeat these rnds once more for rnds 47–54

CHART A

XL

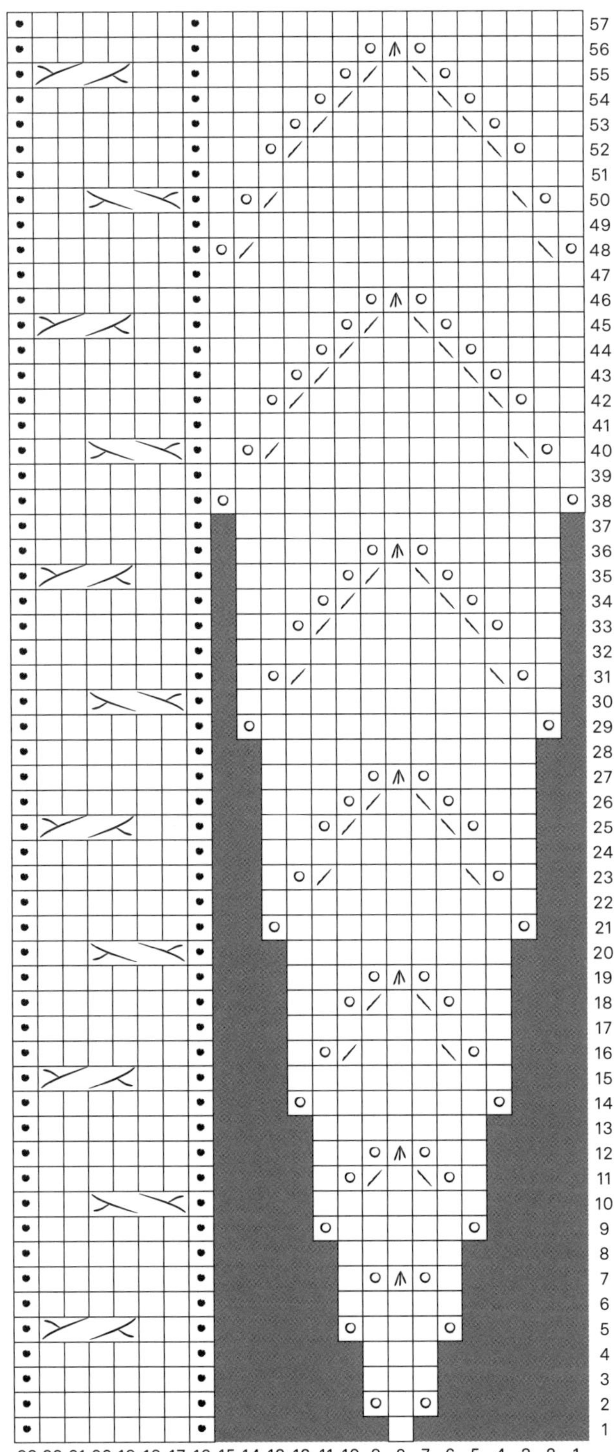

CHART A

2XL

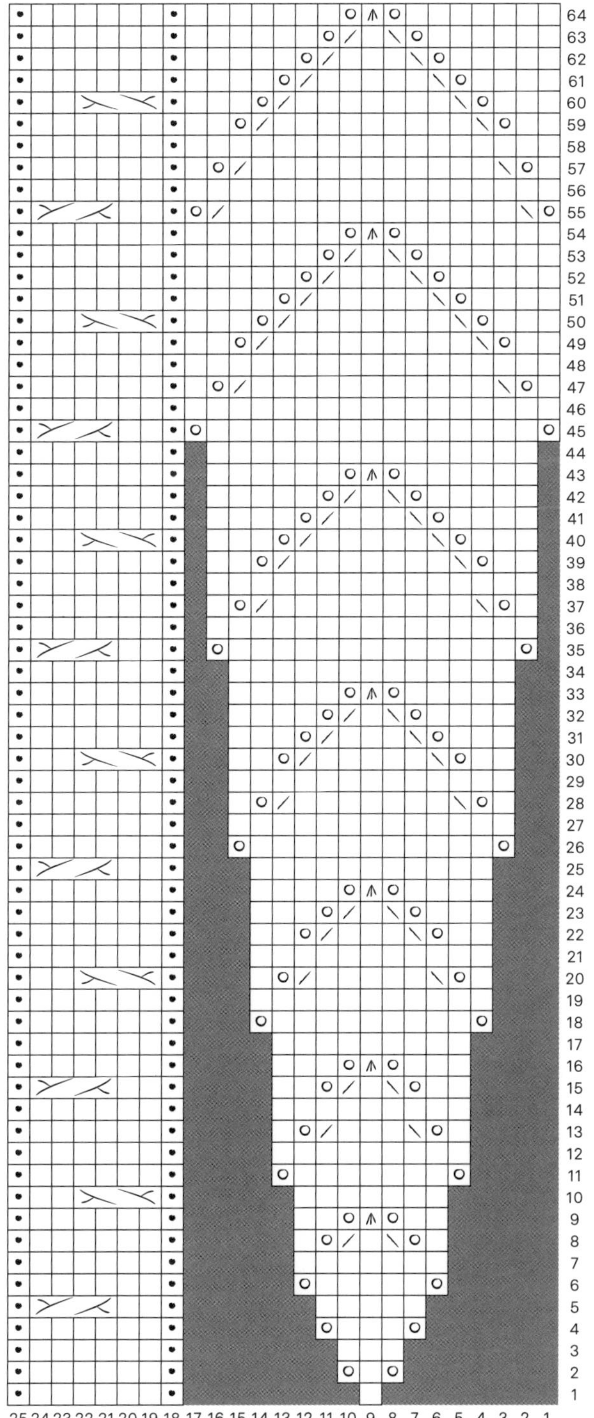

- knit
- purl
- yo
- knit 2 together
- ssk
- 2/2 LC
- 2/2 RC
- slip 1, knit 2 together, pull slipped stitch over k2tog
- no stitch

CHART A

3XL

knit
purl
yo
knit 2 together
ssk
3/3 LC
3/3 RC
slip 1, knit 2 together, pull slipped stitch over k2tog
no stitch
repeat rnds 37–46 two more times for rnds 47–66

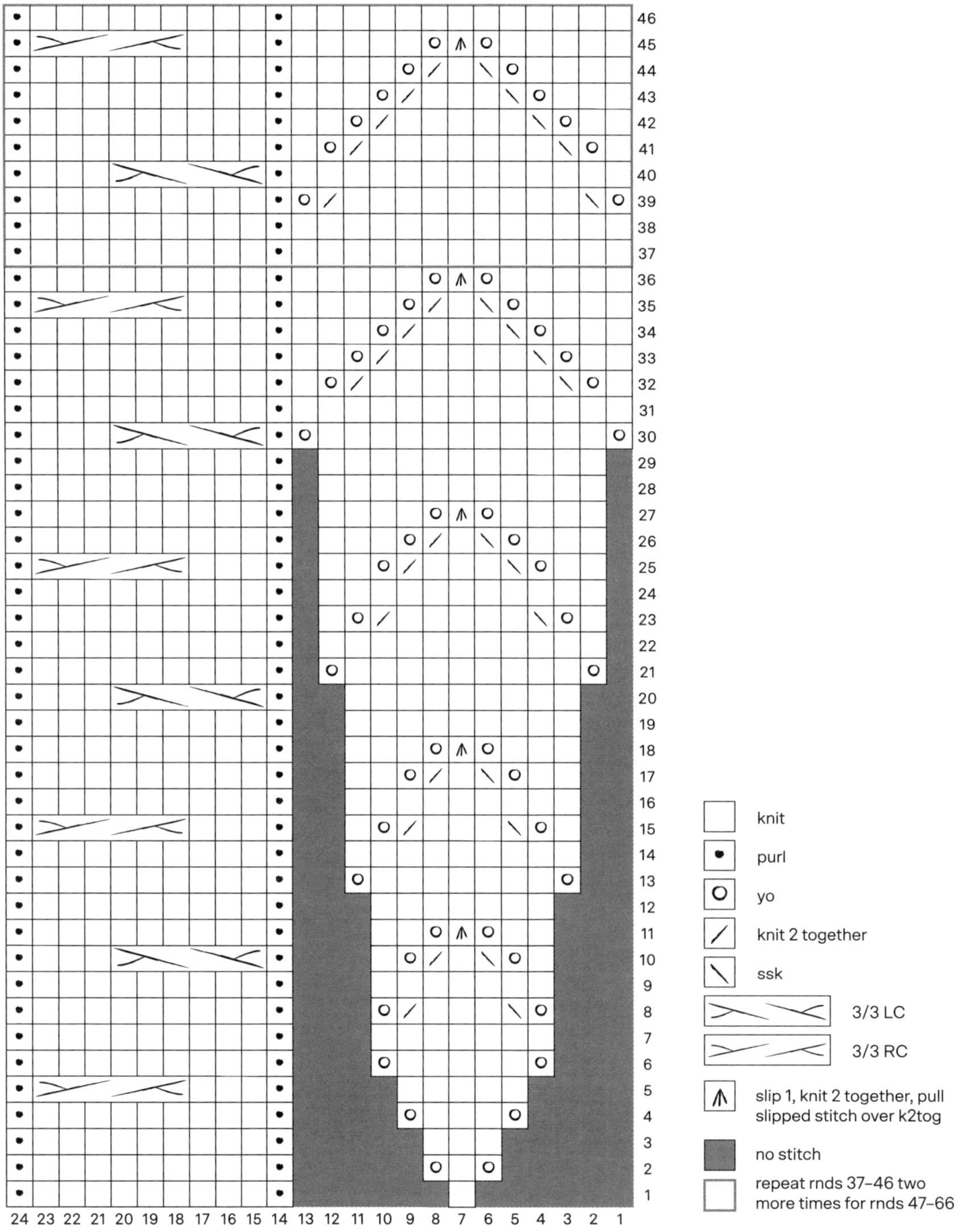

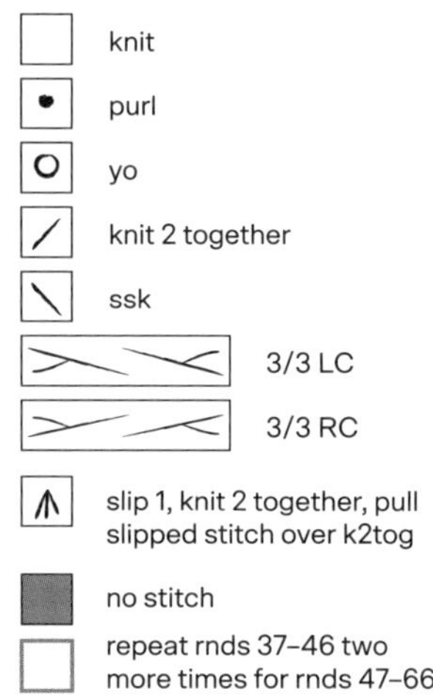

CHART A

4XL

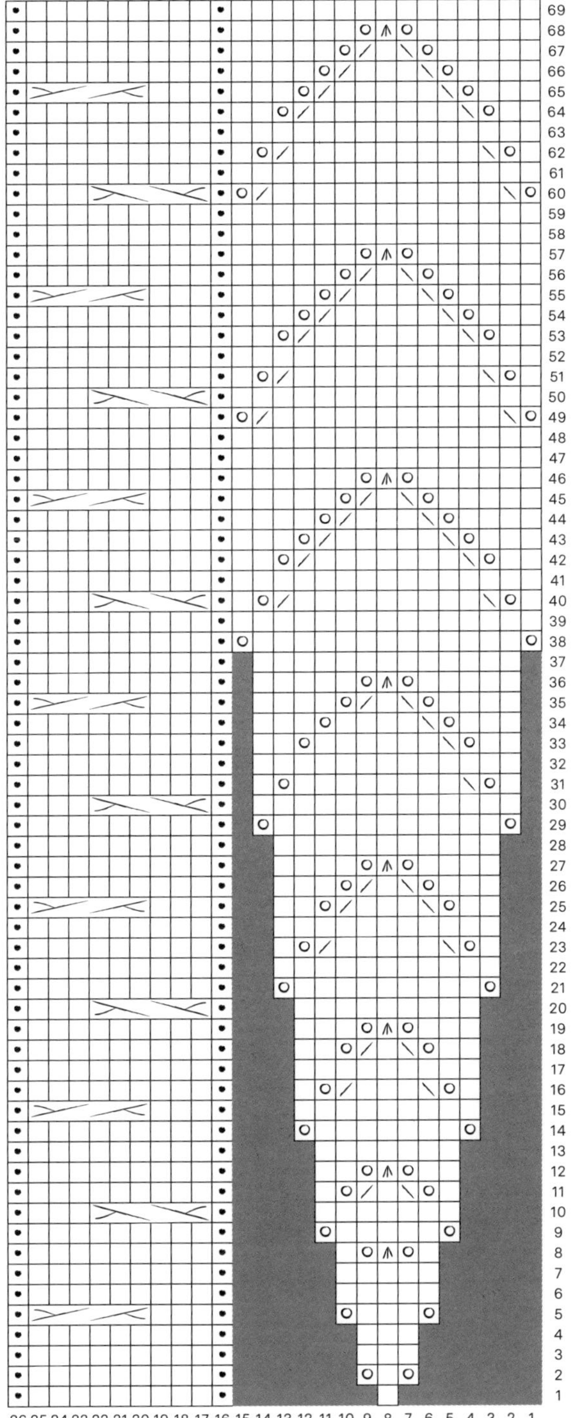

CHART A

5XL

knit
purl
yo
knit 2 together
ssk
3/3 LC
3/3 RC
slip 1, knit 2 together, pull slipped stitch over k2tog
no stitch

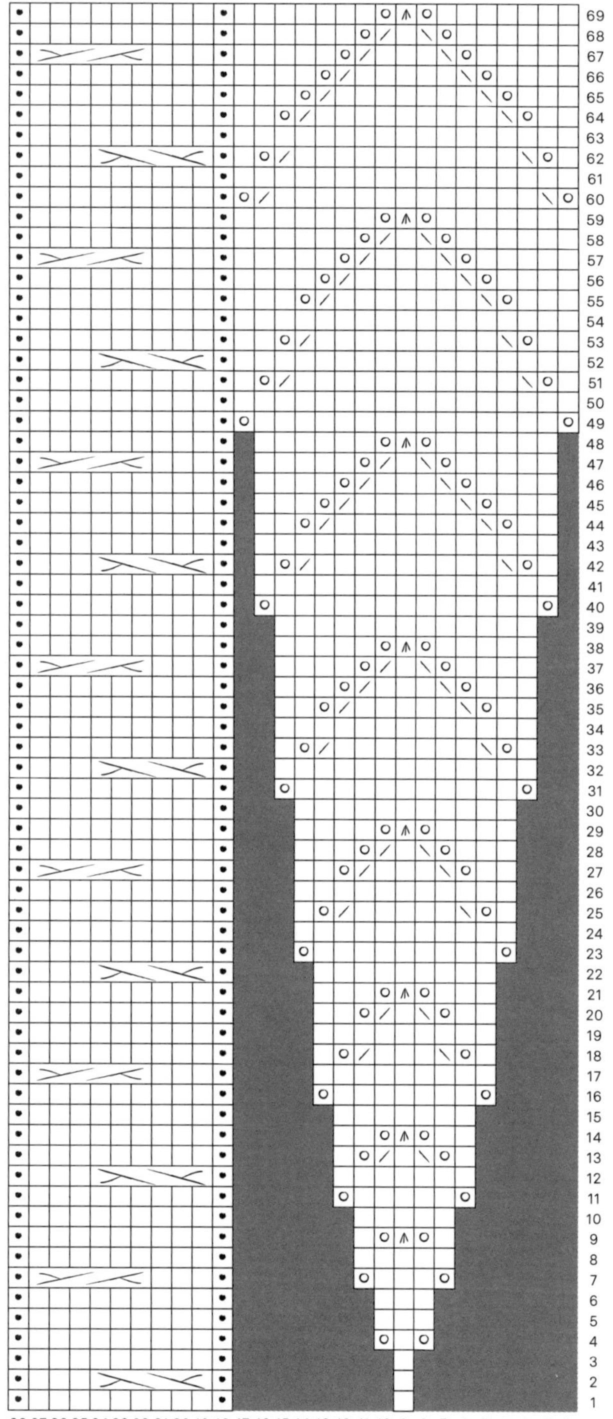

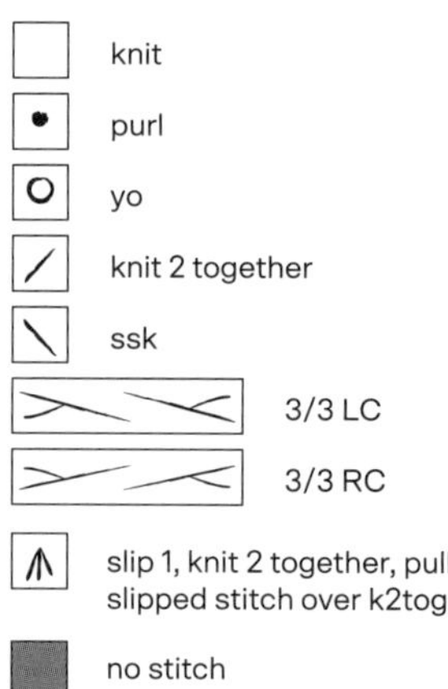

CHART B

XS & L

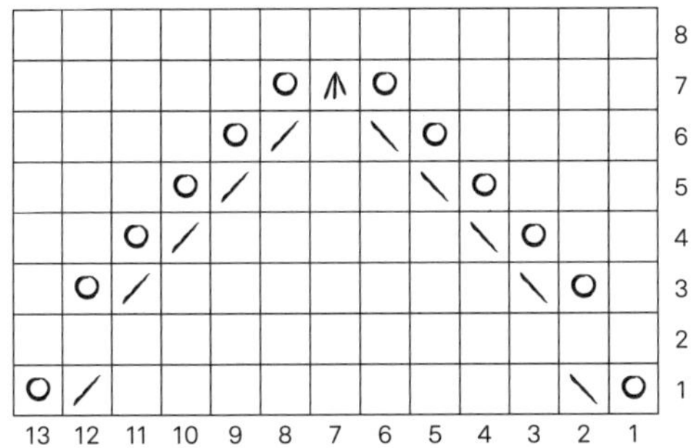

S, XL & 4XL

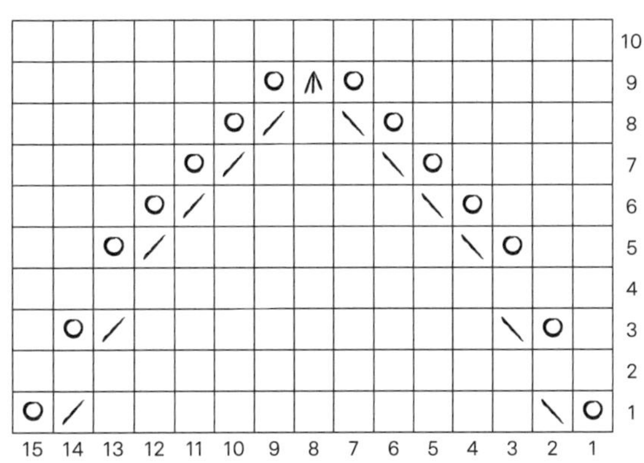

M, 2XL & 5XL

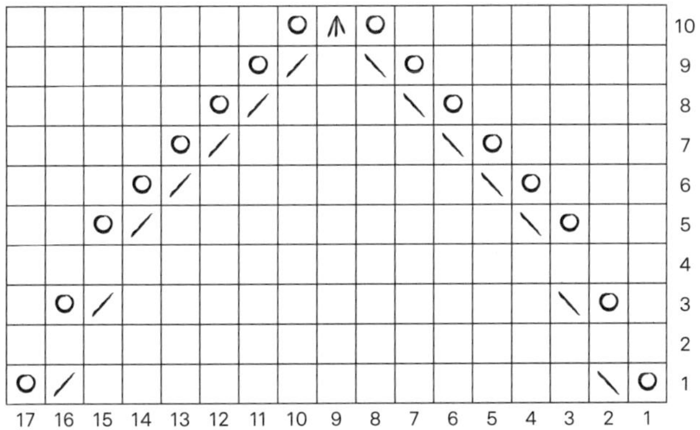

3XL

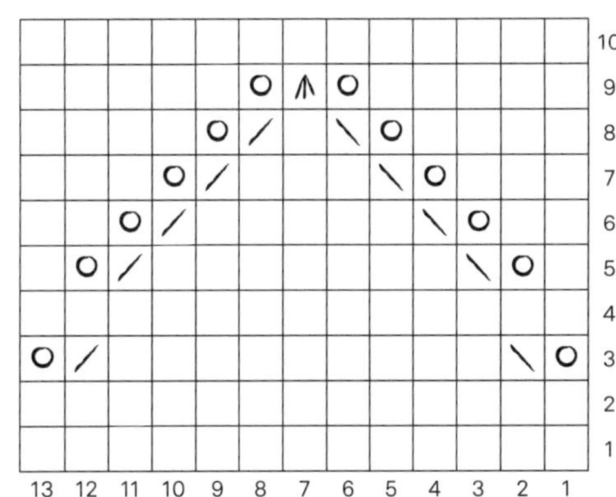

(blank)	knit
•	purl
\	ssk
/	knit 2 together
⋀	slip 1, knit 2 together, pull slipped stitch over k2tog
O	yo

CHART C

S & XL

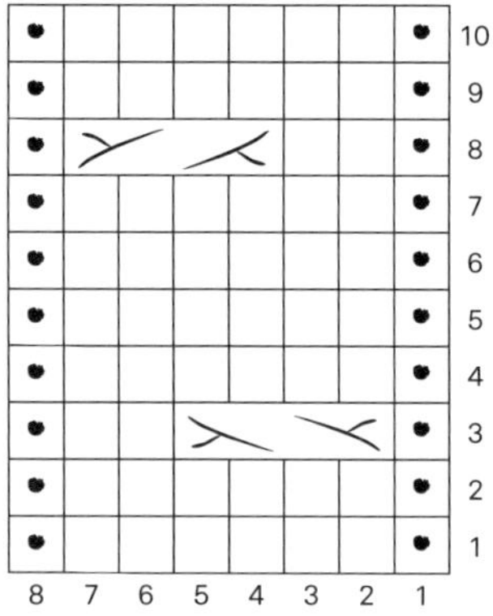

M & 2XL

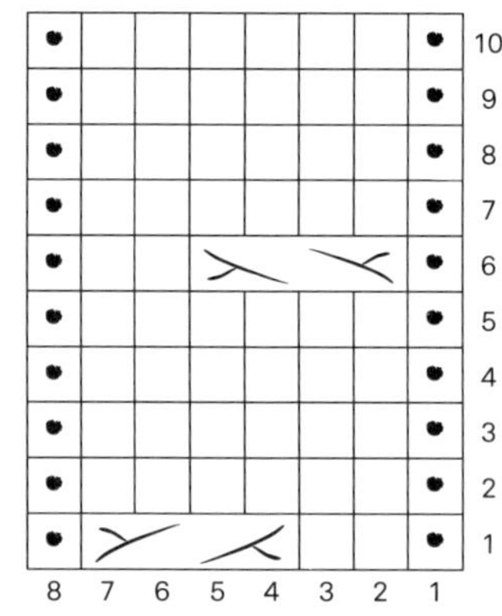

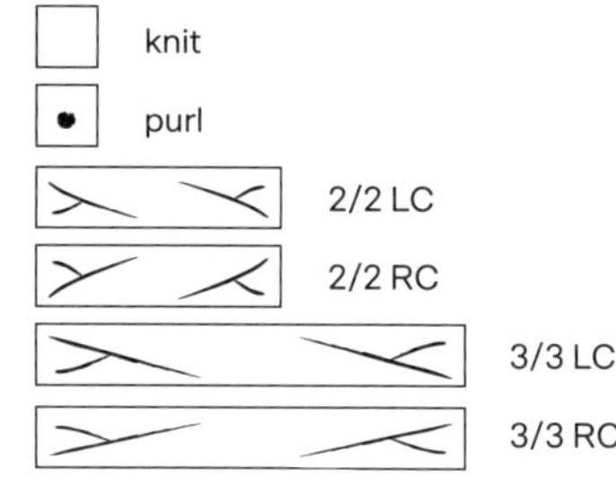

XS & L

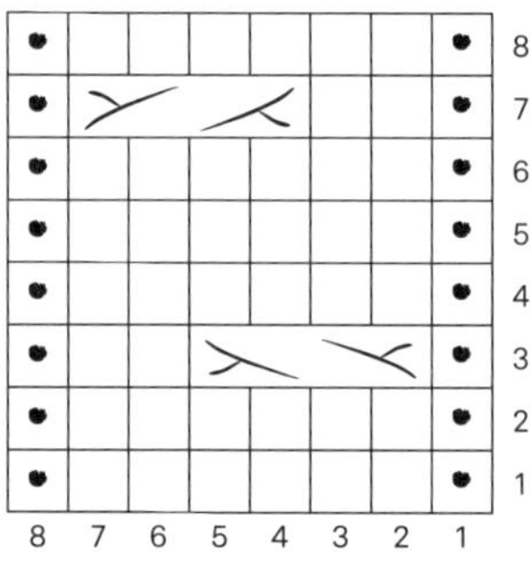

3XL

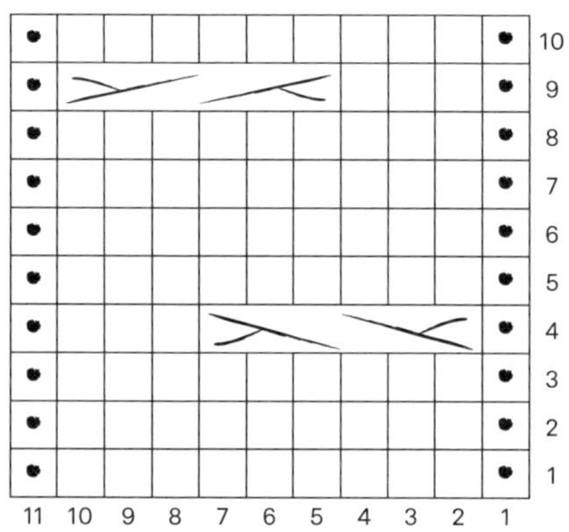

4XL

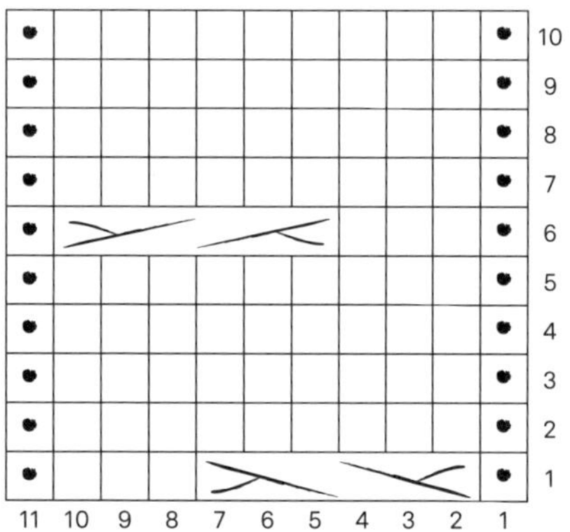

5XL

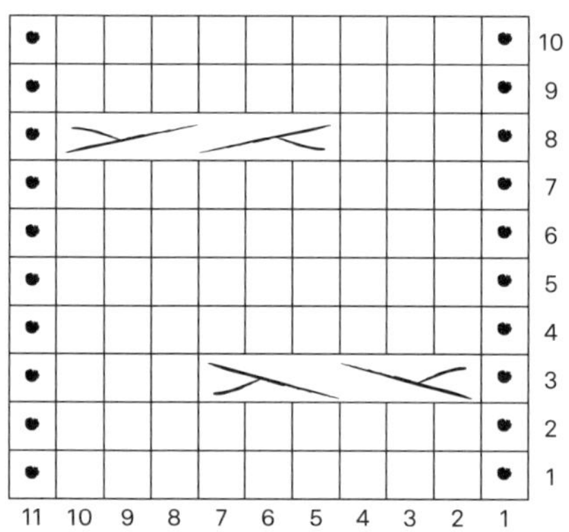

STYLING TIP #12

For a timeless and elegant look, stick to a soft, neutral colour palette that never goes out of style. Elevate the ensemble with a few carefully chosen accessories, embracing the 'less is more' philosophy to add just the right touch of sophistication.

Inspired by balmy days spent outside on a terrace sipping a delicious drink or reading a good book – both occasions when you want to look chic without sacrificing comfort – Send Me a Postcard features a relaxed fit for a laid-back feel. The front neckline has a boatneck-inspired shape that gives the top a polished look, while the scooped back adds an elegant detail. You could even turn the top around and wear it with the back as the front if you want!

SEND ME A POSTCARD

STYLING TIP #13

Create eye-catching contrasts in your outfit by mixing different 'moods' together. Pair a dramatic scooped-back top with casual boyfriend jeans for a down to earth yet striking look. Top it off with a playful accessory like a pearl-embellished headband, and carry a cute bag to add stylish, unexpected elements that make your ensemble pop.

Sizes

XS (S, M, L) (XL, 2XL, 3XL) (4XL, 5XL)

Finished garment measurements

Bust circumference: 82 (92, 100, 110) (118, 126, 136) (144, 154) cm / 32.25 (36.25, 39.5, 43.5) (46.5, 49.5, 53.5) (56.75, 60.5)".

Length from underarm to hem: 30 cm / 12".

The Send Me a Postcard top is designed to have 0–5 cm / 2–4" of negative ease. Sample shown in size S (Kika has a bust of approx. 89 cm / 35").

Gauge

21 sts × 30 rows/rnds = 10 cm / 4" in Stockinette st on 4 mm / US 6 needles, after blocking.

20 sts × 30 rows/rnds = 10 cm / 4" in 1 × 1 rib on 3 mm / US 2.5 needles, after blocking.

Needles

3 mm / US 2.5: circular needles 40–60 cm / 16–24" for I-cord neck opening and armholes, and 80–100 cm / 32–40" for hem rib, and DPN for I-cord.

4 mm / US 6: circular needles 80–100 cm / 32–40" for body.

Notions

Stitch markers, removeable stitch marker, tapestry needle, stitch holder or scrap yarn.

Suggested yarn

The top can be worked with one strand of DK weight yarn or by holding two strands of fingering weight yarn together.

You need approx. 440 (500, 565, 625) (690,750, 815) (875, 1000) m / 481 (547, 618, 684) (755, 820, 891) (957, 1094) yds of DK weight yarn or 875 (1000, 1125, 1250) (1375, 1500, 1625) (1750, 2000) m / 958 (1094, 1230, 1367) (1504, 1640, 1777) (1914, 2187) yds of fingering weight yarn.

Sample knitted with yarns

175 (200, 225, 250) (275, 300, 325) (350, 375) g of Knitting for Olive Pure Silk (100% silk – 250 m / 273 yds / 50g) in the colour Pink Daisy.

The top is worked by holding two strands together.

DIRECTIONS

The top is worked top down seamlessly, you begin by working the front flat and then you pick up stitches for the left and right upper back separately. The upper back is shaped flat and then all stitches are joined to work the body in the round. The armholes and neckline are finished with an I-cord edge.

Upper Front

The Upper Front is worked flat in Stockinette st while shaping the shoulders and armholes.

Cast on 26 (30, 32, 34) (36, 38, 40) (44, 46) sts using the Backwards Loop Cast-On method with 4 mm / US 6 circular needles. Place a removable stitch marker into the first and last st on the needle to mark where sts will be picked up for the left and right back later. **Note!** These markers aren't carried along the work.

Begin shaping the shoulders as follows:
Row 1 (WS): P all sts.
Row 2 (RS): K3, M1L, k to last 3 sts, M1R, k3. 2 sts increased.

Row 3: P3, M1Rp, p to last 3 sts, M1Lp, p3. 2 sts increased.

There are 30 (34, 36, 38) (40, 42, 44) (48, 50) sts in total.

Repeat rows 2–3, 7 (8, 9, 10) (10, 11, 12) (12, 14) more times.

There are 58 (66, 72, 78) (80, 86, 92) (96, 106) sts in total.

Place two additional removable stitch markers into the first and last st on the needle to mark where sts will be picked up for the Left and Right Back later (these markers aren't carried along the work).

Continue working in Stockinette st until the Upper Front measures 10 (11, 11, 12) (13, 13, 14) (14, 15) cm / 4 (4.25, 4.25, 4.75) (5, 5, 5.5) (5.5, 6)" in total from the cast-on edge. End after a WS row with the RS facing for the next row.

Begin shaping the armholes as follows:
Row 1 (RS): K3, M1L, k to last 3 sts, M1R, k3. 2 sts increased.
Row 2 (WS): P all sts.
Row 3: K all sts.
Row 4: P all sts.

There are 60 (68, 74, 80) (82, 88, 94) (98, 108) sts in total.

Repeat rows 1–4, 7 (8, 9, 11) (13, 14, 15) (16, 16) more times.

There are 74 (84, 92, 102) (108, 116, 124) (130, 140) sts in total.

The Upper Front is completed, cut the yarn and let the sts rest while working the Upper Back next.

Upper Left Back

Next, sts are picked up along the left side of the Upper Front to work the Left Back flat. The armhole is shaped by working decreases along the edge and the scooped back is shaped by working increases.

Work as follows: Pick up and k18 (20, 22, 24) (24, 26, 28) (28, 32) sts from the left side stitch marker to the outer edge (when looking at the piece with the RS facing you and the cast-on edge facing up towards the top) with 4 mm / US 6 circular needles, you can remove these markers now.

Begin shaping the shoulder as follows:
Row 1 (WS): P to end.
Row 2 (RS): K to last 5 sts, k2tog, k3. 1 st decreased.
Row 3: P to end.
Row 4: K to end.
Row 5: P to end.

There are 17 (19, 21, 23) (23, 25, 27) (27, 31) sts in total.

Repeat rows 2–5, 3 (3, 3, 4) (4, 4, 5) (5, 5) more times.

There are 14 (16, 18, 19) (19, 21, 22) (22, 26) sts in total.

Work 20 (20, 20, 22) (22, 22, 24) (24, 24) rows of Stockinette st.

Begin shaping the scooped back and armhole as follows:
Row 1 (RS): K3, M1L, k to last 3 sts, M1R, k3. 2 sts increased.
Row 2 (WS): P to end.
Row 3: K3, M1L, k to end. 1 st increased.
Row 4: P to end.

There are 17 (19, 21, 22) (22, 24, 25) (25, 29) sts in total.

Repeat rows 1–4, 3 more times.
There are 26 (28, 30, 31) (31, 33, 34) (34, 38) sts in total.

Cut the yarn and let the sts rest while working the Upper Right Back next.

Upper Right Back

Next, sts are picked up along the right side of the Upper Front to work the Right Back flat.

Work as follows: Pick up and k18 (20, 22, 24) (24, 26, 28) (28, 32) sts from the right outer edge to the right side stitch marker (when looking at the piece with the RS facing you and the cast-on edge facing up towards the top) with 4 mm / US 6 circular needles, you can remove these markers now.

Begin shaping the shoulder as follows:
Row 1 (WS): P to end.
Row 2 (RS): K3, ssk, k to end. 1 st decreased.
Row 2: P to end.
Row 3: K to end.
Row 4: P to end.

There are 17 (19, 21, 23) (23, 25, 27) (27, 31) sts in total.

Repeat rows 1–4, 3 (3, 3, 4) (4, 4, 5) (5, 5) more times.

There are 14 (16, 18, 19) (19, 21, 22) (22, 26) sts in total.

Work 20 (20, 20, 22) (22, 22, 24) (24, 24) rows of Stockinette st.

Begin shaping the scooped back and armhole as follows:

Row 1 (RS): K3, M1L, k to last 3 sts, M1R, k3. 2 sts increased.
Row 2 (WS): P to end.
Row 3: K to last 3 sts, M1R, k3.1 st increased.
Row 4: P to end.

There are 17 (19, 21, 22) (22, 24, 25) (25, 29) sts in total.

Repeat Rows 1–4, 3 more times.

There are 26 (28, 30, 31) (31, 33, 34) (34, 38) sts in total.

Don't cut the yarn yet.

Joining the Upper Right and Upper Left Back

Next, join the Upper Right and Upper Left Back sts on the same circular needle and cast on new sts for the middle of the scooped back.

Work as follows:
Joining row 1 (RS): Upper Right Back sts: K3, M1L, k to end of sts, cast on 16 (18, 22, 24) (26, 26, 28) (30, 30) sts using the Backwards Loop Cast-On method, connect the Upper Left Back sts: k to last 3 sts, M1R, k3. 2 sts increased.

There are 70 (78, 84, 88) (90, 94, 98) (100, 108) sts in total.

Row 2 (WS): P to end.
Row 3 (RS): K to end.
Row 4: P to end.
Row 5: K3, M1L, k to last 3 sts, M1R, k3. 2 sts increased.
Row 6: P to end.
Row 7: K to end.
Row 8: P to end.

There are 72 (80, 86, 90) (92, 96, 100) (102, 110) sts in total.

Repeat rows 5–8, 1 (2, 3, 6) (8, 10, 12) (14, 15) more times.

There are 74 (84, 92, 102) (108, 116, 124) (130, 140) sts in total.

Body

Join the Back and Front sts to form the body on 4 mm / US 6 circular needles (80–100 cm / 32–40") and begin working in the rnd as follows:

Joining rnd 1: K across the 74 (84, 92, 102) (108, 116, 124) (130, 140) sts for the back, cast on 6 (8, 8, 8) (10, 10, 12) (14, 14) sts with the Backwards Loop Cast-On method for the underarm, k across the 74 (84, 92, 102) (108, 116, 124) (130, 140) sts for the front, cast on 6 (8, 8, 8) (10, 10, 12) (14, 14) sts with the Backwards Loop Cast-On method for the underarm, PM (=BOR-m).

There are 160 (184, 200, 220) (236, 252, 272) (288, 308) sts in total.

Work in Stockinette st in the rnd until the body measures 27 cm / 10.5" from underarm (or, until the body measures 3 cm / 1.25" cm less than total desired length).

Change to 3 mm / US 2.5 circular needles and work *k1, p1* rib until the hem measures 3 cm / 1.25". Bind off all sts using the Standard Bind-Off method (or your preferred stretchy bind-off method).

I-cord edges

An I-cord edge is worked around the neckline and both armholes using 3 mm / US 2.5 circular needles and a DPN.

Please note! If you knit very tight you might want to use larger size needles for the I-cord edges and pick up a few extra sts for the collar and armholes.

Collar

With 3 mm / US 2.5 circular needles (40–60 cm / 16–24"), begin at the right shoulder seam when looking at the piece in front of you by picking up and k sts as follows: pick up and k1 for every st from the front cast-on neckline, continue and pick up and k5 sts for every 7 rows from one side of the scooped back (in other words: k3 in every row, skip 1, k2 in every row, skip 1), then pick up and k1 for every st at the back neck cast-on edge, and lastly pick up and k5 for every 7 rows from the other side of the scooped back neck.

Work an I-cord edge as follows:
Cast on 3 new sts on the left needle using the Knitted Cast-On method on the RS.
K2, k2tog tbl, slip 3 sts from the right to the left needle, repeat *–* until there are only 4 sts remaining on the right needle.

Graft the last 4 sts together with the beginning of the I-cord edge so that the join becomes invisible.

Armholes

With 3 mm / US 2.5 (40–60 cm / 16–24") circular needles, start at the middle of the underarm, pick up and k approx. 2 sts for every 3 sts/ rows (in other words: k2, skip 1).

Work an I-cord edge as follows:
Cast on 3 new sts on the left needle using the Knitted Cast-On method on the RS.
K2, k2tog tbl, slip 3 sts from the right to the left needle, repeat *–* until there are only 4 sts remaining on the right needle.

Graft the last 4 sts together with the beginning of the I-cord edge so that the join becomes invisible.

Finishing

Weave in all ends.

Clean lines let the slightly dramatic one-shoulder detail steal the spot-light, making Fortuna the star of the show. This top exudes effortless elegance with its classic design. Adding a touch of playfulness, the top features a simple crochet edge in a contrasting colour around the neckline and armhole, bringing a delightful twist to the otherwise minimalistic style.

FORTUNA

Sizes

XS (S, M, L) (XL, 2XL, 3XL) (4XL, 5XL)

Finished garment measurements

Bust circumference: 71.5 (76, 85.5, 93.5) (105, 114.5, 124) (133.5, 146.5) cm / 28.25 (30, 33.75, 36.75) (41.25, 45, 48.75) (52.5, 57.75)".

Length from underarm to hem: 33.5 (34.5, 34.5, 35.5) (36.5, 36.5, 36.5) (38.5, 38.5) cm / 13.25 (13.5, 13.5, 14) (14.25, 14.25, 14.25) (15.25, 15.25)".

The Fortuna top is designed to have about 10–15 cm / 4–6" negative ease for a tight fit.

Sample shown in size S (Kika has a bust of approx. 89 cm / 35").

Gauge

21 sts × 31 rows/rnds = 10 cm / 4" in Stockinette st on 3.5 mm / US 4 needles, after blocking.

Needles

2.5 mm / US1.5: circular needles 40–60 cm / 16–24" for hem rib.

3.5 mm / US 4: circular needles 60–100 cm / 24–40" for shoulder strap and body.

Notions

4 mm / G-6 crochet hook, tapestry needle, stitch holder or scrap yarn.

Suggested yarn

The top is worked with a sport weight yarn, you need approx.:
MC: 500 (580, 660, 710) (745, 825, 875) (910, 960) m / 547 (635, 723, 776) (815, 902, 956) (995, 1049) yds of sport weight yarn.
CC: 33 m / 37 yds of sport weight yarn.

Sample knitted with yarns

MC: 150 (150, 175, 200) (225, 250, 275) (300, 325) g of Hjertegarn Cotton nr. 8 (100% cotton – 165 m / 180 yds per 50 g) in the colour 199.
CC (crochet edge): 10 g of Hjertegarn Cotton nr. 8 in the colour 201.

DIRECTIONS

This top is worked seamlessly from the top down. You'll start by knitting the back of the shoulder strap flat, then pick up stitches from the top of the shoulder to work the front strap flat. Once the front and back straps are joined, additional stitches are cast on to shape the body, which is worked in the round. To finish, a contrasting crochet edge is added along the neckline and armhole, completing the look with a chic flourish.

Back Shoulder Strap

The Back Shoulder strap is worked flat in Stockinette st, then sts are picked up from the cast-on edge to work the Front Shoulder strap.

Cast on 12 (14, 14, 14) (16, 16, 16) (18, 18) sts using the Backwards Loop Cast-On method with 3.5 mm / US 4 circular needles or double pointed needles.

Work one set-up row as follows:
Set-up row (WS): P all sts.
Continue working in Stockinette st until the shoulder strap measures 10 cm / 4" from the cast-on edge, ending with the RS facing for the next row.

Start shaping the neckline of the shoulder strap as follows:
Row 1 (RS): K2, M1L, k to end. 1 st increased.
Row 2 (WS): P to end.
Row 3: K to end.
Row 4: P to end.
Rows 5-8: Repeat rows 1–4 once more.

There are 14 (16, 16, 16) (18, 18, 18) (20, 20) sts in total.

Continue shaping the neckline as follows:
Row 9 (RS): K2, M1L, k to end. 1 st increased.
Row 10 (WS): P to end.
Rows 11-16: Repeat rows 9–10, 3 more times.

There are 18 (20, 20, 20) (22, 22, 22) (24, 24) sts in total.

Continue shaping the neckline as follows:
Row 17 (RS): K2, M1L, k to end. 1 st increased.
Row 18 (WS): P to last 2 sts, M1Lp, p2. 1 st increased.
Rows 19-24: Repeat rows 17–18, 3 more times.

There are 26 (28, 28, 28) (30, 30, 30) (32, 32) sts in total.

Continue shaping the neckline and begin shaping the armhole as follows:
Row 25 (RS): K2, M1L, k to last 2 sts, M1R, k2. 2 sts increased.
Row 26 (WS): P2, M1Rp, p to last 2 sts, M1Lp, p2. 2 sts increased.
Rows 27-28: Repeat rows 25–26 once more.

There are 34 (36, 36, 36) (38, 38, 38) (40, 40) sts in total.

Cut the yarn and leave the sts on hold while working the front of the shoulder strap next.

Front Shoulder Strap

Facing the RS, pick up and k12 (14, 14, 14) (16, 16, 16) (18, 18) sts with 3.5 mm / US 4 circular needles from the cast-on edge of the Back Shoulder strap.

Work one set-up row as follows:
Set-up row (WS): P all sts.

Work in Stockinette st until the shoulder strap measures 10 cm / 4" from the cast-on edge.

Start shaping the neckline of the shoulder strap as follows:
Row 1 (RS): K to last 2 sts, M1R, k2. 1 st increased.
Row 2 (WS): P to end.
Row 3: K to end.
Row 4: P to end.
Rows 5-8: Repeat rows 1–4 once more.

There are 14 (16, 16, 16) (18, 18, 18) (20, 20) sts in total.

Continue shaping the neckline as follows:
Row 9 (RS): K to last 2 sts, M1R, k2. 1 st increased.
Row 10 (WS): P to end.
Rows 11-16: Repeat Rows 9–10, 3 more times.

There are 18 (20, 20, 20) (22, 22, 22) (24, 24) sts in total.

Continue shaping the neckline as follows:
Row 17 (RS): K to last 2 sts, M1R, k2. 1 st increased.
Row 18 (WS): P2, M1Rp, p to end. 1 st increased.
Rows 19-24: Repeat rows 17–18, 3 more times.

There are 26 (28, 28, 28) (30, 30, 30) (32, 32) sts in total.

Continue shaping the neckline and begin shaping the armhole as follows:

Row 25 (RS): K2, M1L, k to last 2 sts, M1R, k2. 2 sts increased.
Row 26 (WS): P2, M1Rp, p to last 2 sts, M1Lp, p2. 2 sts increased.
Rows 27-28: Repeat rows 25–26 once more.

There are 34 (36, 36, 36) (38, 38, 38) (40, 40) sts in total.

Don't cut the yarn yet.

Body

Next, join the Back and Front Shoulder straps and cast on new sts for the lower body.

Work as follows:
Row 1 (RS): K34 (36, 36, 36) (38, 38, 38) (40, 40) Front Shoulder Strap sts, cast on 64 (68, 86, 100) (118, 138, 156) (172, 198) sts with the Backwards Loop Cast-On method for the neckline, connect the Back Shoulder Strap sts that were on hold and k34 (36, 36, 36) (38, 38, 38) (40, 40) sts, cast on 18 (20, 22, 24) (26, 26, 28) (28, 30) sts with the Backwards Loop Cast-On method for the underarm. Place marker to indicate beginning of rnd (=BOR-m).

There are 150 (160, 180, 196) (220, 240, 260) (280, 308) sts in total.

Work in Stockinette st in the rnd until the top measures 31 (32, 32, 33) (34, 34, 34) (36, 36) cm / 12.25 (12.5, 12.5, 13) (13.5, 13.5, 13.5) (14, 14)" from the cast-on edge (or until the top measures 2.5 cm / 1" less than total desired length).

Change to 2.5 mm / US 1.5 circular needles and work *k1 tbl, p1* rib until the hem measures 2.5 cm / 1".

Bind off using the Standard Bind-Off method (or your preferred stretchy bind-off method).

Crochet edges

A crochet edge is worked around the neckline and the armhole.

With crochet hook 4 mm / G-6 and the contrasting-coloured yarn: work a rnd of single crochet sts as follows: work 1 single crochet in approx. every second row along the shoulder straps and 1 single crochet in every knitted st along the neckline and armhole.

Finishing

Weave in all ends.

STYLING TIP #14

Add a touch of glitz to your outfit by wearing a statement piece of jewellery that instantly catches the eye. Whether it's a bold necklace or sparkling earrings, it's like the cherry on top that transforms your look from simple to simply stunning.

Knit in a dense alpaca-bouclé combination, the Fuzz It vest has structure and a put-together look. It's the perfect garment to wear when it's too hot for a full woolly sweater, yet you still want to add a touch of warmth and attitude to your outfit. Worked on large needles, this vest is a quick and fun project. It's versatile enough to be worn as outerwear or indoors when the season gets cold.

FUZZ IT

WEEKEND

Sizes

XS (S, M, L) (XL, 2XL, 3XL) (4XL, 5XL)

Finished garment measurements

Bust circumference (including front edge plackets when worn open, each approx. 3 cm / 1.25"): 92 (100, 108, 116) (126, 132, 142) (148, 158) cm / 36.25 (39.25, 42.5, 45.75) (49.5, 52, 55.75) (58.25, 62.25)".

Body length from underarm to hem: 30.5 cm / 12" (or desired length).

The Fuzz It vest is designed to have 10–20 cm / 4–8" of positive ease, if you're between two sizes I recommend choosing the larger size.

Sample shown in size M (Kika has a bust of approx. 89 cm / 35").

Gauge

10 sts × 16 rows = 10 cm / 4" in Stockinette st on 6 mm / US 10 needles, after blocking.

Needles

5 mm / US 8: circular needles 60–100 cm / 24–40" for hem rib and front edge plackets, DPN for double knitted front edge plackets. 6 mm / US 10: circular needles 60–100 cm / 24–40" for body.

Notions

Stitch markers, tapestry needle, stitch holder or scrap yarn, 6 sets of snap buttons 1.5 cm / 5/8 diameter.

Suggested yarn

The vest can be worked with one strand of chunky / bulky weight yarn, or with a combination of three strands of worsted / aran weight yarns held together.

You need approx. 170 (175, 185, 200) (210, 230, 245) (255, 270) m / 186 (191, 202, 219) (230, 252, 268) (279, 295) yds of chunky / bulky weight yarn or 1010 (1050, 1115, 1175) (1260, 1365, 1470) (1535, 1600) m / 1105 (1148, 1220, 1285) (1379, 1493, 1608) (1679, 1750) yds of worsted / aran weight yarn.

Sample knitted with yarn

240 (250, 265, 280) (300, 325, 350) (365, 380) g Drops Alpaca Bouclé (80% alpaca, 15% wool, 5% polyamide – 140 m / 153 yds / 50 g) in the colour 0100 **together with** 135 (140, 150, 155) (170, 180, 195) (205, 215) g of Isager Eco Soft (56% alpaca, 44% organic cotton – 125 m / 137 yds / 50 g) in the colour E0.

The vest is worked by holding two strands of alpaca bouclé and one strand of blown alpaca yarn together.

DIRECTIONS

The vest is worked top down flat. First the upper back is worked while shaping the armholes, stitches are then picked up from the shoulders and each upper front is worked separately. All stitches are then joined together to work the body. A double knitted button band is worked along each front edge separately and lastly stitches are picked up from around the neckline for the ribbed double folded collar.

Upper Back

The Upper Back is worked flat. On the first row, removable stitch markers are placed on either side of the neckline to mark where sts will be picked up for the Upper Left and Right Front later.

Cast on 32 (36, 40, 44) (48, 50, 54) (56, 60) sts using the Backwards Loop Cast-On method (or your preferred cast-on method) with 6 mm / US 10 circular needles.

Work as follows:
Row 1 (RS): K11 (12, 12, 14) (15, 16, 18) (19, 20) (= shoulder sts), place a removable marker around the strand between the sts, k10 (12, 16, 16) (18, 18, 18) (18, 20) (= back neck sts), place a removable marker around the strand between the sts, k all remaining 11 (12, 12, 14) (15, 16, 18) (19, 20) (= shoulder sts). **Note!** These markers aren't carried along the work.

Row 2 (WS): P to end.

Continue working in Stockinette st until work measures 16 cm / 6.5" in total from cast-on edge.

Start shaping the armholes as follows:
Row 1 (RS): K2, M1L, k to last 2 sts, M1R, k2. 2 sts increased.
Row 2 (WS): P to end.
Row 3: K to end.
Row 4: P to end.

There are 34 (38, 42, 46) (50, 52, 56) (58, 62) sts in total.

Repeat rows 1–4, 2 more times.

There are 38 (42, 46, 50) (54, 56, 60) (62, 66) sts in total.

Cut the yarn and leave the Upper Back sts to rest while working the Right and Left Upper Fronts.

Right Upper Front

Pick up and k11 (12, 12, 14) (15, 16, 18) (19, 20) sts from the right outer edge to the right side stitch marker (when looking at the piece with the RS facing you and the cast-on edge facing up towards the top) with 6 mm / US 10 circular needles, you can remove this marker now.

Work in Stockinette st flat until the Right Upper Front measures 10 cm / 4" in total from the pick-up edge. End on a WS row (so that the next row is a RS row).

Begin shaping the neckline by working increases, work as follows:

Row 1 (RS): K to last 2 sts, M1R, k2. 1 st increased.
Row 2 (WS): P to end.

Repeat rows 1–2, 2 more times.

There are 14 (15, 15, 17) (18, 19, 21) (22, 23) sts in total.

Cast on new sts for the neckline on the following row and begin shaping the armhole.

Work as follows:
Row 1 (RS): K2, M1L, k to end, cast on 2 (3, 5, 5) (5, 6, 6) (6, 7) sts with the Backwards Loop Cast-On method and place a removable stitch marker into the last st (this is to mark where sts will be picked up for the double knitted front edge placket later).
Row 2 (WS): P to end.

There are 17 (19, 21, 23) (24, 26, 28) (29, 31) sts in total.

Row 3: K to end.
Row 4: P to end.
Row 5: K2, M1L, k to end. 1 st increased.
Row 6: P to end.
Row 7: K to end.
Row 8: P to end.

There are 18 (20, 22, 24) (25, 27, 29) (30, 32) sts in total.

Repeat rows 5–6 once more.

There are 19 (21, 23, 25) (26, 28, 30) (31, 33) sts in total.

Cut the yarn and leave the sts to rest as you work the Left Upper Front next.

Left Upper Front

Pick up and k11 (12, 12, 14) (15, 16, 18) (19, 20) sts from the left side stitch marker to the outer edge (when looking at the piece with the RS facing you and the cast on edge facing up towards the top) with 6 mm / US 10 circular needles, you can remove this marker now.

Work in Stockinette st flat until the Left Upper Front measures 10 cm / 4" in total from the pick-up edge. End on a WS row (so that the next row is a RS row).

Begin shaping the neckline by working increases, work as follows:

Row 1 (RS): K2, M1L, k to end. 1 st increased.
Row 2 (WS): P to end.

Repeat rows 1–2, 2 more times.

There are 14 (15, 15, 17) (18, 19, 21) (22, 23) sts in total.

Cast on new sts for the neckline on the following row and begin shaping the armhole.

Work as follows:
Row 1 (RS): K to last 2 sts, M1R, k2. 1 st increased.
Row 2 (WS): P to end, cast on 2 (3, 5, 5) (5, 6, 6) (6, 7) sts with the Backwards Loop Cast-On method and place a removable stitch marker into the last st (this is to mark where sts will be picked up for the double knitted front edge placket later).

There are 17 (19, 21, 23) (24, 26, 28) (29, 31) sts in total.

Row 3 (RS): K to end.
Row 4 (WS): P to end.
Row 5: K to last 2 sts, M1R, k2. 1 st increased.
Row 6: P to end.
Row 7: K to end.
Row 8: P to end.

There are 18 (20, 22, 24) (25, 27, 29) (30, 32) sts in total.

Repeat rows 5–6 once more.

There are 19 (21, 23, 25) (26, 28, 30) (31, 33) sts in total.

Don't cut the yarn.

Joining the Upper Fronts with the Upper Back

Next, connect the Upper Back sts with the Left and Right Upper Front sts and cast on new sts for the underarms. Work as follows:

Row 1 (RS): K to end of the Left Upper Front sts, cast on 5 (5, 5, 5) (6, 7, 8) (9, 10) sts with the Backwards Loop Cast-On method, connect the Upper Back sts that were on hold and k to end, cast on 5 (5, 5, 5) (6, 7, 8) (9, 10) sts with the Backwards Loop Cast-On method, connect the Right Upper Front sts and k to end.

There are 86 (94, 102, 110) (120, 126, 136) (142, 152) sts in total.

Body

Work in Stockinette st flat until the body measures 28 cm / 11" from the underarm (or until the body measures 2.5 cm / 1" less than total desired length).

Change to 5 mm / US 8 circular needles and work *k1, p1* rib until the hem measures 2.5 cm / 1" in total. Bind off all sts using the Standard Bind-Off method.

Front edge plackets

For the front edge placket sts are picked up along the front edges with 5 mm / US 8 circular needles. The front edge placket is worked in double knitting with 5 mm / US 8 double-pointed needles.

Left Front Edge
Start by picking up and knitting sts as follows:

Pick up and k1 in every row along the left front edge starting at the bottom left side (when looking at the vest with the front and RS facing you) to the stitch marker placed when casting on sts for the neckline. The amount of picked up sts will depend on how long your vest is. Cut the yarn and remove the marker.

Join in new yarn and begin working the double knitted placket from the bottom left front edge.

Work as follows:
Turn the work so that the WS is facing you. With the 5 mm / US 8 circular needles, and using the Italian cast-on method, cast on 9 new sts in addition to the picked up sts, making the first and last st of the cast on sts purl sts. Turn the work so that the RS is facing you and work as follows:

Row 1 (RS): *K1, sl1 wyif*, repeat from * to * a total of 4 times, k2tog tbl (k the last st of the 9 sts that you just cast on together with the first st from the picked up sts through the back loops). Turn work.
Row 2 (WS): *Sl1 wyif, k1*, repeat from * to * to the last st, sl1 wyif. Turn work.

Repeat rows 1–2 across all the picked up sts along the left front edge until there is only 1 of the picked-up sts left (until there are only 10 sts remaining on the needle).

Bind off from the RS using the Italian Bind-Off method. When working the last 2 sts of the Italian Bind-Off, seam these 2 sts as if they were 1 st (i.e., as if you had knitted them together tbl).

Right Front Edge
Start by picking up and knitting sts as follows:

Pick up and k1 in every row along the right front edge starting at the stitch marker placed when casting on sts for the neckline to the bottom right side (when looking at the vest with the front and RS facing you). The amount of picked up sts will depend on how long your vest is. Cut the yarn and remove the marker.

Join in new yarn and start working the double knitted placket from the top right front edge.

Work as follows:
Turn the work so that the WS is facing you. With the 5 mm / US 8 circular needles and using the Italian cast-on method, cast on 9 new sts on in addition to the picked up sts, make the first and last st of the cast on sts purl sts. Turn the work so that the RS is facing you and work as follows:

Row 1 (RS): *K1, sl1 wyif*, repeat from * to * a total of 4 times, k2tog tbl (k the last st of the 9 sts that you just cast on together with the first st from the picked up sts through the back loops). Turn work.
Row 2 (WS): *Sl1 wyif, k1*, repeat from * to * to the last st, sl1 wyif. Turn work.

Repeat rows 1–2 across all the picked up sts along the left front edge until there is only 1 of the picked-up sts left (until there are only 10 sts remaining on the needle).

Bind off from the RS using the Italian Bind-Off method. When working the last 2 sts of the Italian Bind-Off, seam these 2 sts as if they were 1 st (as if you had knitted them together tbl).

Collar

With 5 mm / US 8 (60–80 cm / 24–32") circular needles pick up and k79 (81, 83, 85) (87, 89, 91) (93, 95) sts from the neckline (including the double knitted front edge plackets).

Row 1 (WS): P1, *p1, k1* to the last 2 st, p1, p1.
Row 2 (RS): K1, *k1, p1* to the last 2 sts, k1, k1.

Repeat rows 1–2 until the collar measures 10 cm / 4" in total.

Bind off loosely using the Standard Bind-Off method.

Finishing

Fold the collar double and attach it on the inside by hand sewing.

Spread out the 6 press buttons evenly along one of the front edge plackets by placing the bottom and top snap button approx. 1 cm / 0.5" from the hem and collar edge, and spacing out the 4 remaining snap buttons evenly. Attach the bottom piece of each snap button by hand sewing and then attach the corresponding top part of each press button on the backside of the other front placket edge, making sure the buttons on the front and back align with each other.

STYLING TIP #15

Pair your fuzzy vest with a shirt featuring decorative details to instantly add texture and visual interest to your outfit. The soft fuzziness of the vest contrasts beautifully with the intricate elements of the shirt, creating a look that's both cosy and stylish.

A knitted collar is a charming accessory that adds a playful, romantic touch to your outfit. Worked in a beautiful lace stitch pattern, Yours Truly features a cute ribbon detail on the front as a delightful finishing touch. This collar is a great 'one-skein project', allowing you to use random leftover yarns or skeins from your stash. It's also perfect for those looking for something quick or wanting to knit a gift for someone.

YOURS TRULY

STYLING TIP #16

Combine the Yours Truly collar with a textured knit, like the My Favourite Story sweater, pattern on pages 48–63.

Sizes
One size.

Finished measurements

Collar upper edge length: 46 cm / 18".

Collar bottom edge length: 84 cm / 34.25".

Gauge

19 sts × 30 rows/rnds = 10 cm / 4" in pattern lace stitch on 3 mm / US 2.5 needles, after blocking.

Needles

3 mm / US 2: circular needles 60–100 cm / 24–40" and 2 DPNs for I-cord tie string.

Notions

Tapestry needle.

Suggested yarn

The collar is worked in a DK weight yarn, you need approx.: 110 m / 120 yds of DK weight yarn.

Sample knitted with yarn

50 g of Sandnes Garn Line (53% cotton, 33% viscose, 14% linen – 110 m / 120 yds / 50 g) in the colour 3511.

DIRECTIONS

The collar is worked flat bottom up. Decreases are incorporated into the lace stitch pattern to create the collar shaping. An I-cord tie string is worked separately and attached to the collar. First the left side of the I-cord tie string is worked, then it's attached to the collar and the I-cord edge of the collar is worked, and lastly the right side of the tie string is worked.

Collar

Cast on 159 sts with the Italian Cast-On method (or your preferred stretchy cast-on method) on 3 mm / US 2.5 circular needles.

Row 1 (RS): K1, work row 1 of Chart A until the last st (chart repeats 8 times), k1.
Row 2 (WS): Sl1 wyif, work the next row of Chart A, p1.
Row 3: Sl1 wyib, work the next row of Chart A until the last st, k1.

Continue working in the same manner, always working the next row of Chart A until all rows 1–31 are completed.

There are 87 sts in total.

Leave the sts on hold on the circular needles while working the I-cord tie string.

I-cord edge and tie string

The left side of the I-cord tie string is first worked separately, then it's attached to the collar and the I-cord edge of the collar is worked, and lastly the right side of the tie string is worked.

Left side I-cord tie string

With a 3 mm / US 2.5 DPN, cast on 3 sts using the Knitted Cast-On method. Begin working the left side of the I-cord tie string as follows:

Row A: Slide all 3 sts from the left side of the DPN to the right side and k3.

Repeat row A until the I-cord measures 37 cm / 15" in total.

Collar I-cord edge

Attach the I-cord tie string to the collar as follows:

Row B: Slide all 3 sts from the left side of the DPN to the right side, k2, k2tog tbl (k the last st of the I-cord tie string together with the first st from the collar sts through the back loops)

Repeat row B until all of the collar sts are worked.

Right side I-cord tie string

Work the right side of the I-cord tie string by repeating row A until the right side of the I-cord measures 37 cm / 15" in total, then k3tog and pull yarn through.

Finishing

Weave in all ends.

CHART A

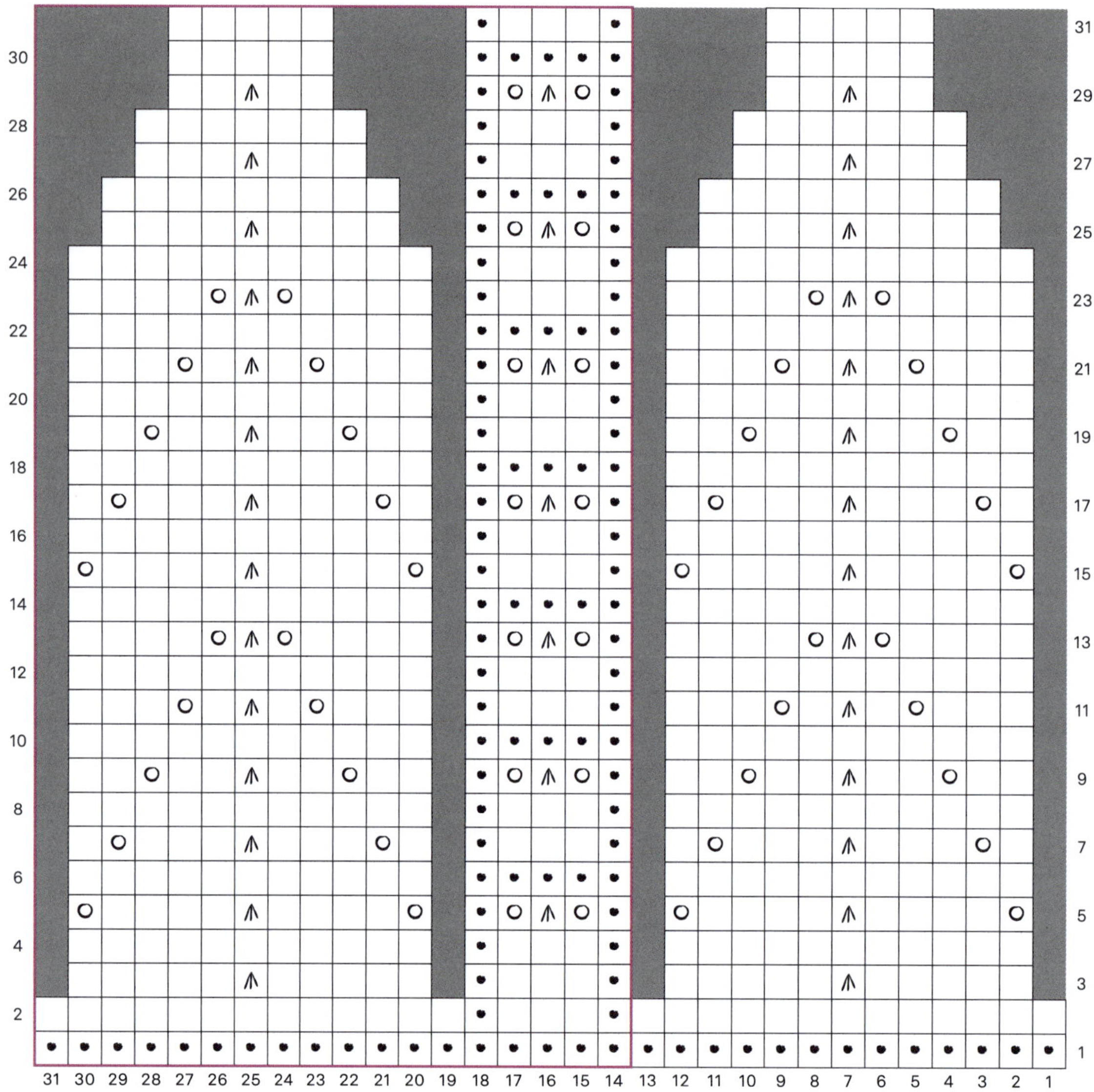

rs: knit, ws: purl

• rs: purl, ws: knit

O yo

⋀ slip 1, knit 2 together, pull slipped stitch over k2tog

no stitch

pattern repeat

STYLING TIP #17

Mix things up by layering your lace collar over a sharp, tailored shirt to add contrast to your look. The juxtaposition of delicate and soft lace against the crisp lines of the shirt creates a balance that's both feminine and edgy, giving your outfit a unique twist that's sure to turn heads.

Delightfully plump and cosy, this hat is worked in a simple cable stitch pattern, making it perfect for chilly days when you want both warmth and style. Its rich texture and snug fit make Twist It an ideal accessory for outdoor adventures, whether you're taking a brisk walk in the woods or heading out for brunch with friends.

TWIST IT

SCHULZ BY CROWD

STYLING TIP #18

Top off your outfit with a chunky beanie for a cosy yet cool and street-smart look. The beanie adds warmth and texture, making your ensemble both practical and stylish, whether you're strolling through the city or hanging out with friends. Kika is wearing the Simple Things sweater in pink, pattern on pages 34–41.

Sizes

One size.

Finished garment measurements

Brim circumference:
47 cm / 18.5".

Total length without folded brim:
41 cm / 16".

Total length with folded brim:
23.5 cm / 9.25".

The beanie is designed to have about 8–12 cm / 3–4.75" of negative ease as the fabric will stretch out quite a bit when worn.

Gauge

20 sts × 20 rnds = 10 cm / 4" on 5 mm / US 8 needles in Chart A cable pattern, after blocking when the fabric is relaxed and not stretched out.

17 sts × 21 rnds = 10 cm / 4" on 4 mm / US 6 needles in 1 × 1 rib, after blocking when the fabric is relaxed and not stretched out.

Needles

4 mm / US 6: circular needles 40–60 cm / 16–24" (or longer ones for the Magic Loop technique) for rib.

5 mm / US 8: circular needles 40–60 cm / 16–24" (or longer ones for the Magic Loop technique) and DPNs for crown shaping if you're not using the Magic Loop technique.

Notions

Stitch markers, tapestry needle.

Suggested yarn

The beanie is worked by holding one strand of worsted weight yarn together with two strands of lace weight yarn. You need approx. 125 m / 137 yds of worsted weight yarn and 450 m / 492 yds of lace weight yarn.

Sample knitted with yarn

50 g of Knitting for Olive Heavy Merino (100% merino wool – 125 m / 137 yds / 50 g) in the colour Powder **together with** 25 g of Knitting for Olive Silk Mohair (70% mohair, 30% silk – 225 m / 246 yds / 25g) in the colour Powder **together with** 25 g of Knitting for Olive Silk Mohair in the colour Cloud.

The beanie is worked by holding one strand of merino and two strands of silk mohair together.

DIRECTIONS

The beanie is worked bottom up in the round. The brim is worked in a 1×1 rib and folded twice. The crown is shaped by working decreases.

Brim

Cast on 80 sts with the Backwards Loop Cast-On method with 4 mm / US 6 circular needles. Join in the rnd and place BOR-m.

Work *k1, p1* rib until the beanie measures 7.5 cm / 3" in total.

First fold: Work one rnd of k sts. This will create a rnd of purl sts on the outside which will help the fold to stay in place neatly.

Second fold: Then work *k1, p1* rib until the beanie measures 10 cm / 4" from the first fold (or, until the beanie measures 17.5 cm / 7" in total) and work one more rnd of k sts for the second fold.

Work *k1, p1* rib until beanie measures 8.5 cm / 3.25" from the second fold (or until the beanie measures 26 cm / 10.25" in total).

Beanie

Change to 5 mm / US 8 circular needles and begin working according to Chart A across all sts (Chart A repeats 8 times across all sts).

Work rnds 1–4 of Chart A a total of 6 times. Then work rnds 1–2 of Chart A.

Shaping the crown

You might want to change to 5 mm / US 8 DPNs to shape the crown of the beanie if you're not using the Magic Loop technique here.

Rnd 1: *Ssk, k2tog, p1* to end of rnd.

There are 60 sts in total.

Rnds 2–3: *K2, p1* to end of rnd.
Rnd 4: *K2tog, p1* to end of rnd.

There are 40 sts in total.

Cut the yarns and pull through all the live sts. Thread the yarns onto a tapestry needle and pull them tight so that the crown opening shuts close.

Finishing

Weave in all ends and fold up the brim double.

CHART A

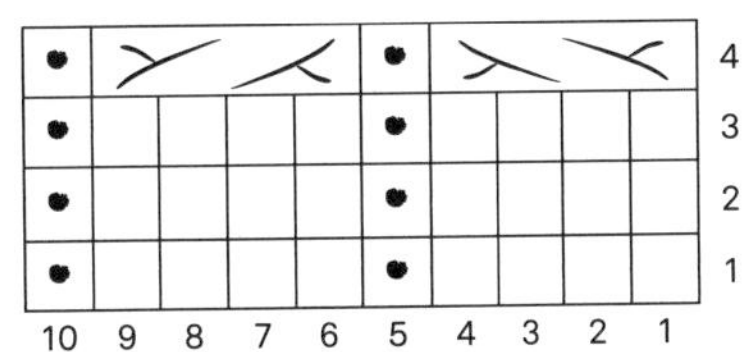

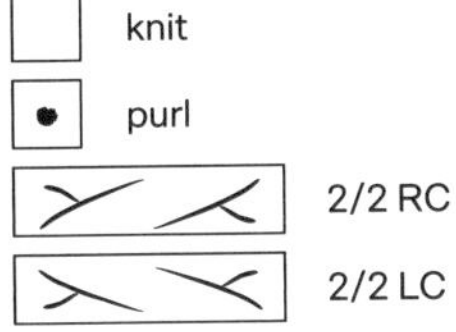

THANK YOU

They say that writing a book is like giving birth to a baby. Well, when I was making this book, I also had an *actual* baby. So as you can imagine, I've needed all the support I could get to bring this this book to life while navigating life as a new mum.

A huge thank you to my dear family, I would never have been able to pull it all together without you. Thank you, Juki, Mum and my little sister, for following along to Copenhagen and helping me behind the scenes so we could take all the photos for this book, you are a dream team!

Thank you to the talented sample knitters who helped knit the garments for this book: Suvi Cederberg, Emma Gylling, Jenni Kuutti, Outi Loukola, Essi Malismaa, Elise Matleena and Elisa Seppänen. Thank you for your precise technical pattern editing, Melinda Measor and Jesslyn Di Fiori. Thank you, Kelsey, for helping me organise the test knits, and thank you to all the test knitters around the world for your time, effort and feedback in helping me try out these patterns.

Thank you, Jonna, Pauliina and Sini and the entire Laine team, it's been a joy to work with such a dedicated and skilful group of professionals. Thank you for your vision and beautiful layout, Anna-Mari.

Thank you to my dear friends and colleagues Suvi, Sari and Leeni, for inspiring me and always being ready to share your advice and wisdom.

TEST KNITTERS

Sydney Mantrom, Noêmi Ribeiro, Patrycja Zajda @leaf_and_stitch, Lily Yommer, Zoya @knits_gone_rogue, Kahilah Harry, Aislinn Friedman, Friederike Kara Vieten, Clara Lepp, Kirsi Lehtola, Jessika Preuß-Werner, Sabryn Vanhoose, Laetitia Van Parys, Conor S., Chanel Hsei, Nicole Sano, Molly Lunderville, Carina Liebeknecht, Lauren Macpherson, Stephanie Woolever, Ilse Maes, Sandra Moeys (sandys_moois), Holle Wade, Imke S., Sabine Mangold, Ausrine Bereniene aka @shpokaknits, Birgit Beck, Rachel Williams-Giordano, Silvia Wenter, Almedina Cuskic, Liz Larson, Ona Sauliene, Lina Weimers Durgé, Anna Syrjänen @annan_neuleet, Anniek Schriever, Corinne Nilsen, Julia Schulte, Monica Hopkins, Jeanet Lindås, Nana M., Elizabeth Molyneaux, Anna Nowak - Sploty na fali, Risa Ishikawa, Misha Suksnguan, Elizabeth Johnny, Friederike Lasch, Kirsi Lehtola, Kiera Insetta, Mary Ellen Stjerne, Faith Smith, Hannah Bourn, Heidi Iik, Luna Meyer-Fredrich, Caty Waterman, Evelinn Idenfors, Beverly Hess, Justyna Pieniążek, José Repko - de Vries, Carina Herrling, Sabrina Wong, Kiia Arola, Chanel Hsei, Adeline Lum, Tine Tacq, Claudia Stockhaus, Tanja Lehtonen, Mayte Lorenzo, Rachachel Juanita Applevich, Dóri Krasznai, Sarah I. Garry, Svannah Morse, Martina Neumeier, Hanna Bruzi, Dana Weber, Jessica Meyers, Maggie Raczkowska, Erminia Angilletta, José Repko - de Vries (@Jrdv_knitting), Minna Puonti, Tori Brown, Ashley Pigott, @Oonawknits, Marina Ramos, Vanity Behr, Liesel Kuhn, Swantje Caliebe, Marisa Skowronski, Senja Elizabeth, Nina Johansson, Katherine Trull, Emily Bell, Lotta Pirttimäki, Haley Hulsey, Alicia Rubiales, Kelly Bohl, Sara Kangasniemi, Parkring, Emma Andersson, Chanel Hsei, Edith Marroquin, Sabine Mangold, Joanna Filip @joann.fil, Agnese Linarts, Fadak: knitknatss, Elizabeth Villalobos (@knittingforwolves), Leena Lindfors, Jill M. Smith, Tracy Clark, Lori Beekman, Agata Kriegel, Mélody de Graaf, Deifilia Kieckhefen, Olga Suomalainen, Roosa Varjus, Gintare Kiseliene, Nathalie S, Heike Kirmse, Lila Farwell, Fay Downer, Tania Pais, Frenzie Torres, Helen Jo Zitzmann, Tania Valenti, Victoria Thomas, Anna Nowak - sploty_na_fali, Nicole Xia, Kiia Arola, Laura Alanko, Sierra Armién Funk, Linda Westfall, Susan Blair, Holle Wade, Mollie Melba, Sally Kim, Mariana Costa, Sun van Helvoort (@Sunneke), Brittany Trotter, Mila27, Anaïs Kakrow, Zuzanna Pabin (on_her_needles), Martina Neumeier, Josefine Kark, Mara Schröder, Mattea Chadwick, Deborah Mandy Wren, Sonia Kaminska, Elizabeth Johnny, Julie Hyldgaard Frisk, Chloe Cheng, Monika Biedermann, Michelle Bucknall, Ilse Maes, Rachel Williams-Giordano, Ciara Bergmann (@cexoxoma_knits), Lena Dziuba, Zeina Abdallah, Marta Antão, Colleen M. Davis, Joanne Grochowski, Liesel Kuhn, Maggie Ritchie, Elise Otti, Anne Missel, Ana Rei, Haley Hulsey, Emma Morrice, Angelique @skalarknits, Elsa Genet, Sophia Klymchuk, Kirsten5macs, Jane Wirawan (JWMakes), Sara Koskiniemi, Tatiana Zhurova, Júlia Lolbert-Szabó, Svitlana Sasaga, Lan Nguyen, NikeKnits, Cynthia Chi, Alka Shah, Abigail Feeley, Emily Bell, Sara Kangasniemi, Senta v. Münchow, Stephanie Woolever, Mary-Lou Korf (Strandstrick), Nora of NorArt, Gosia (Beginner Crafter), Selena Boutilier, Sarah Nap, Barbara Kuipers, Marta Tyniec, Ro Crawford, Ashley Enriquez (ashyknitting), Sonja Kilpatrick, Jennifer Barr, Tina Baumgartner, Joan Porter, Shelly Neiman, Courtney Shea, Lucy Grover (Ravelry: Handmade Knitwear)

This edition published in 2026 by Hardie Grant Books, an imprint of Hardie Grant Publishing
First published in 2024 by Laine Publishing Oy
Published by arrangement with Rights & Brands

Hardie Grant Books (Melbourne)
Wurundjeri Country
Level 11, 36 Wellington Street
Collingwood, Victoria 3066

Hardie Grant North America
2912 Telegraph Ave
Berkeley, California 94705

hardiegrant.com/books

A catalogue record for this book is available from the National Library of Australia

Knits to Wear
ISBN 978 1 76145 223 9

10 9 8 7 6 5 4 3 2 1

Text & patterns: Veronika Lindberg
Photography: Veronika Lindberg, Jukka Heino, Rebecka Lindberg
Graphic design: Anna-Mari Tenhunen
Models: Veronika Lindberg, Jukka Heino, Rebecka Lindberg

Colour reproduction by Splitting Image Colour Studio
Printed Printed in China by Leo Paper Products LTD.

The paper this book is printed on is from FSC®-certified forests and other sources. FSC® promotes environmentally responsible, socially beneficial and economically viable management of the world's forests.